David C. Brubaker

ecology
and
man

D0402081

This book is printed on paper containing a substantial amount of recycled fiber. The paper has been supplied by the Wausau Paper Company of Wausau, Wisconsin.

In addition to making considerable use of recycled fiber, Wausau is one of the first major paper mills to develop the high temperature recovery process of paper making chemicals. Their recovery process has contributed greatly to pollution abatement of the Wisconsin river—a problem of grave concern to environmentalists.

ecology
and
man

REZNEAT M. DARNELL

Texas A&M University

WM. C. BROWN COMPANY PUBLISHERS

Dubuque, Iowa

credits

Stewart L. Udall. "A Message for Biologists." *BioScience*, November, 1964, pp. 17–18.

Rezneat M. Darnell. "A Declaration of Dependence." Bioscience, September 1, 1970, p. 945.

Wm. D. Ruckelshaus. Address to the American Chemical Society. September 13, 1971.

Alice F. Jackson and Bettina. "Autobiography of James Albert Jackson, Sr., M.D." Wisconsin Magazine of History, Vol. 28, No. 1 (Sept. 1944), p. 25.

Consulting Editor
E. Peter Volpe
Tulane University

Printed in the United States of America

To those species
of plants and animals
Which have vanished
by the hand of man,
To the native American
flora and fauna,
Lest they be forgotten—

contents

foreword

Ecology, discovered belatedly by the public, is an environmental science. Ecologists study living communities; their interactions with one another and with the chemical and physical world. Ecologists not only try to understand nature but to manage it for man's use and enjoyment. Today's ecologists who are over thirty years of age have observed a deterioration of landscapes within their own lifetime; hence, they are worried and conscious of their responsibility to those generations which follow ours.

Professor Rezneat Darnell is one of these concerned ecologists. He expresses it through an understanding of nature's processes as exemplified in this book and by public service through his activities in organizations which work toward the improvement of environmental quality or for preservation of native communities or species.

In Wisconsin he served selflessly as a member and chairman of the Wisconsin Scientific Areas Preservation Council. Over the years, his knowledge, conviction, and forthright action led to setting aside over twoscore unique areas in which plant and animal species can be studied by future generations of scholars and enjoyed by citizens who will find them a source of esthetic beauty as well as a place to gain satisfaction in learning nature's secrets through careful observation.

Some will differ with Rezneat Darnell about his choice of ecological examples selected for teaching purposes. These are the ones he knows best as exemplified by the contagious enthusiasm of his prose. It is well done.

Ecology is a young science, but it is already so important that it is now appropriate subject matter for every college student. In fact, it is, in my opinion, as essential for cultural background as a course in European history. Because, in order to vote intelligently today, everyone needs a basic understanding of ecology. Upon the integrity of ecosystems rests the vitality of our living environment which sustains our food and fiber resources free of charge. If man's activities destroy these systems, it will cost us dearly to grow substitute crops of fish and trees with man-made artificial systems.

The traditional natural sciences such as chemistry and physics have increased our knowledge through the scientific method by conducting experiments which control all variables except one in evaluating cause and effect. In ecological studies this technique is inadequate because of the many factors operating simultaneously in an ecosystem. Discovering explanations for the functioning of an ecosystem is far more complex. It will be necessary for the next generation of ecologists to develop new techniques for evaluating cause and effect in nature. Present methods lack the precision we need to predict the effect of man's technology on ecosystems. This book will serve well to develop a cadre of students who, I hope, will accept the challenge to learn what we now know and to apply that knowledge to the solution of our growing ecological problems through development of innovative techniques and procedures for deciphering the functioning of the natural systems and predicting the outcome of man-made changes. In order to live abundantly and with dignity, we must know how. Darnell's book can guide our hopeful youth.

A. D. Hasler
Professor of Zoology and
Director, Laboratory of Limnology, University of Wisconsin
Director, The Institute of Ecology

preface

I have attempted in these few chapters to treat the field of ecology, both in its subject content and in its pervasive implications for human society. I have tried with subdued strokes to paint ecology as a science, but more than that, as a bridge between science and humanism. The public message of modern ecology involves elements of both philosophy and science. For this I offer no apology. But I am deeply concerned that, hampered by subject-oriented training and communication skills sieved through years of specialized investigation and terse technological writing, I may have proven inadequate to the task of transmitting an important message beyond the audience of my worried colleagues.

The message had already been received by a young lady in Taiwan who recently wrote inquiring about the possibility of carrying out graduate study under my direction.

"... I appreciate that my professors give me so good chance to develop my interest. But the more you learn, the more you want to learn. Meantime, I find that the Current Ecology is no more the Ecology which we studied in school. Ecology seems to be everything widespreadly under the background of our basic knowledge in Ecology...."

No one, to my knowledge, has ever expressed it better than Judy. There is the body of principles forming the solid foundation of the basic science of ecology, and there are the recently-evolved volatile, action-oriented, public-issue implications whose roots are grounded in the basic foundation principles, but whose branches reach into the atmosphere of everyday civilization. Science touches society in many ways, but the ecology-environmental issues raised in the past few years have written a unique chapter in history, overshadowing even the nuclear-war conscience which preceded the ecology movement.

The book is divided into two sections. Part I treats the basic principles which govern the world of nature. Part II deals with man as reflected in nature. When I began the task of writing Part II, I had anticipated detailed discussions of the deteriorating quality of human life—the ghettos of Harlem, the high-rise "human filing cabinets" of Long Island, crime in the street, the downtown traffic, social and racial unrest, the freeways, smog, the rising decibel level, the dehumanization of man. As the work proceeded, however, it became clear that other writers are more knowledgeable on these topics and more capable of handling such discussions. My message must derive largely from my own unique experience. Since nature is what I know best, my case must rest largely in this realm. By restricting the scope of my attention, hopefully, I have been able to provide a depth of insight into certain important problems which have been treated only superficially by other recent writers. Taken as a whole, the book displays a single theme: the interdependence of man and nature.

Much of this book could not have been written even two years ago. We are just now reaching the point where we have pulled together the information to provide both historical and global perspective on the roots and extent of the environmental problems. It has been a considerable challenge for the author to obtain the most recent and most authoritative information available, to assimilate this information, and to set it down in relatively nontechnical fashion. In retrospect, the greatest challenge has been to limit the size of the book while still giving adequate coverage to the most important topics.

It must be said that a great deal has been left out and that to be really informed the reader must go beyond these pages, following up the carefully chosen bibliographies given at the end of each chapter. The environmental issues will be with us for a long time to come, and regardless of one's calling in life, as a professional and as a citizen he is well advised to become ecologically informed.

To the students, colleagues, clergymen, regional planners, lawyers, legislators, and private citizens who through the years have influenced my thinking on environmental matters, I extend heart-felt thanks. All have contributed, in some way, to the quality and scope of this work. The entire manuscript has been read by Dr. Grover C. Stephens and Dr. E. Peter Volpe, whose comments have been especially valuable and whose counsel is most appreciated. Dr. Orie L. Loucks kindly provided excerpts from the Constitution of the State of Wisconsin (quoted in Chapter 10). To Jeanne and Molly for inspiration and understanding, words are inadequate to express thanks. The manuscript has been typed by Mrs. Chris McCarthy and Mrs. Gayle Langley whose cheerful and efficient labors have greatly lightened my own. The writing and the artwork were completed by the author, who also accepts responsibility for whatever inadequacies appear between these covers.

Rezneat M. Darnell

I

the

natural

systems

prologue/a glimpse

of nature

The Setting

Dawn in the jungle. The first rays of morning stream across the eastern plains and kindle the mist-enshrouded mountains which tower above our camp. These are the majestic Sierra Madres rising abruptly from the plain a mile to our west. Below the forest canopy, we stir in our jungle hammocks, and water droplets, remnants of the night's downpour, fall to the wet soil. Last evening the moisture-laden winds from the Gulf of Mexico piled clouds against the mountain wall, and this evening they will do the same. Here, below the Tropic of Cancer, the nightly rain is a regular affair during the late spring months, and the dense tropical vegetation which flourishes at the base of the Sierra owes its existence to the high humidity and heavy seasonal precipitation. Only a few miles to the east, the coastal plains are clothed with low scrub vegetation (cacti, mesquite, acacias, and other thorny shrubs), but here at the foot of the mountains the forest is tall and green, trailing with vine-like lianas and liberally sprinkled with mosses, ferns, lichens, orchids, pineapple-like bromeliads, and other air plants. This morning all is dripping wet.

We arise promptly. Sleep is out of the question, for in the treetops the birds have begun to voice their prelude to the day—doves, parrots, guans, trogons, motmots, raucous chachalacas, strident macaws, each with its characteristic call, now melodious, now harmonious, now discordant and vain. What conversations do they make with each other and with the world below? We dress. The warm, damp air bears a heavy organic odor overlaid with the fragrance of a thousand tropical flowers. Or is there just a single orchid, hidden in the airy castle of some tree limb, which permeates our Eden with a delicacy unknown to the outside world?

From the old sugar mill where our hammocks are tied, we proceed down through the cypresses to the nearby stream to wash the night from our eyes, and to drink. No water is so pure, so clear and sweet as that which stems from the Sierra. Back up the riverbank to prepare breakfast. Powdered milk with river water, powdered eggs, hard rolls and jam, and a cup of hot coffee. A hearty breakfast. We also pack a lunch, for today we will make an all-day trip upstream through the canyon to the big spring where the river takes origin, full-blown, from the Sierra. A few half-cooked tortillas pursed over a bit of scrambled eggs and chili peppers will do the trick.

Tidying up the campsite, we notice a coral snake—a graceful but deadly little creature—emerging from a nearby hole. Since we are studying the ecology of the riverbanks as well as the stream, we capture the snake and dispatch it with a strong preservative (formaldehyde) injected into the brain cavity. To achieve good penetration of the preservative we cut through the abdomen and are surprised to discover in the stomach a worm snake in good condition—apparently just consumed. Cutting this open we find an earthworm which, in turn, contains decomposing leaf matter. In a few moments we have witnessed a *food chain* — leaf detritus, to worm, to worm snake, to coral snake. Though two steps removed, the coral snake is ultimately dependent upon the trees for its nourishment.

The Stream

With knapsacks on our shoulders we leave camp and follow the foot trail which leads north along the top of the river bluff for several hundred yards before winding down the bank to where the river is easily forded. Here we pause to inspect the floodplain. Overnight the stream rose and covered a portion of the rocky beach. Receding, it left behind several isolated ponds, some containing small fishes. These we readily recognize as species which are sold in aquarium stores of the larger cities, but who among the hobbyists has seen them in nature? Farther up the bank, we note giant fig trees with extensive systems of gnarled roots extending out among the rocks and boulders. The strangling fig tree begins life as a bird-deposited seed high in the branches of some unfortunate host tree. Growing attachments to the tree, the young fig sends aerial shoots to the ground below where they take root. Growing around and finally encompassing the host tree, the fig prevents its further growth. The host dies and decomposes leaving a hollow core which the fig tree eventually seals.

But the fig tree, in turn, is host to another species. Our attention is drawn to the trunk of one where columns of parasol ants pass up and down in orderly columns. Each descending ant bears a moon-shaped piece of leaf neatly bowed over its head like the brim of an old-fashioned bonnet. These bits of leaf, carefully cut from the tree's canopy, will be stored in subterranean galleries where these agricultural ants cultivate their crops of vegetable molds. As the ants meet, they touch antennae, passing recognition signals known only to themselves.

Moving to the river we inspect the nearby riffle where the stream narrows and flows swiftly over a bed of potato-sized rocks. Each is carpeted with a thin, slippery layer of filamentous algae, and much riverborne debris has lodged in the upstream crevices. The only fish in evidence are small cichlids which feed upon the snails so abundant on the rocky surfaces. Deeper crevices of the riffles shelter a surprising variety of aquatic insect larvae (mayflies, stoneflies, caddis flies, black flies, beetles, etc.) and a peculiar little tropical shrimp. These invertebrates feed upon the filamentous algae, upon the riverborne debris, and upon each other. Together they form a small community of grazers, browsers, and predators. Upstream the river includes a series of such riffles alternating with deeper, wider pool areas, each with its characteristic inhabitants. The pools act as settling basins, and the riffles serve as filters. Together they maintain the clarity and purity of the water which we drank for breakfast and which we shall drink again several times during our day's journey.

Trip to the Headwater Spring

After wading the stream, we climb the far bank and resume our north-ward course along the narrow, shaded jungle trail with its vines, palms, ferns, and large-leaved aroids, seen only in greenhouses of the north. The sun is higher in the sky. Bird songs have ceased, save for the occasional alarm cry of some individual disturbed in the forest. We pad silently along listen-ing for sounds above the low hum of the forest insects, alert to the unexpect-ed, which we have learned may appear just around the next bend of the trail. From time to time we notice new odors, but being citydwellers, we are not attuned to their meanings in a wild world. At first we pass familiar landmarks. Here is where I saw the boa constrictor. There is where I caught the deadly fer-de-lance snake, the northernmost record for the species. Yonder lives a long-tailed laemanctus lizard, relative of the iguana. Some-times we pass close to the stream and notice water lilies growing along the edge of a long pool. Dragonflies sail above, singly or in pairs, straining small insects from the air or perching momentarily upon a water lily. Other times the trail takes us away from the stream, although we may hear the gurgling riffles at a distance.

We have been walking for over an hour, and our leg muscles make us realize that we have been climbing. Limestone outcrops occasionally appear in the bed of the trail, evidence that the soil is becoming thinner. The dense forest has given way to bushes and scrubby trees. In the sunny open patches, lizards scurry across the trail and disappear into the marginal brush. We pass tropical nettle plants in bloom and take care not to brush the prickly leaves. Thorny acacias become the predominant vegetation of the rocky soil. We stop to inspect a bull-horn acacia with its thick, paired spines. Thumping one of the spines, we note the tiny black ants which appear from holes near the thorny tips. The ant and the tree have become working partners through eons of mutual evolutionary history. The tree provides housing, and the ants presumably afford some measure of protec-tion from insect parasites and grazing mammals.

Entering the upper canyon, the trail has become quite rocky, and our attention turns to the remarkable geological features on display. We are in a geosynclinal valley, and the rocky layers are tilted as though for our inspection. The thin-bedded limestones are overlaid with blue and brown shale deposits which crack and crumble into sharp, angular gravel. Occasionally there is a giant conglomerate boulder made of gravel cemented together by natural forces many eons ago in the bed of the ancestral stream. We are hot and a bit fatigued from our climb. The newness has worn off and with it the acute edge of our jungle alertness. Plodding along, our thoughts wander back home to the university.

Rounding a bend, we are suddenly confronted by a pair of large, dark wild animals scuffling only a few yards ahead. Involuntarily we jump and sense the surge of adrenalin to our extremities. Senses suddenly acute, we are alert to a new danger. To remain or to flee is the uppermost question. Our minds quickly eliminate the possibility of jaguars or mountain lions, both of which abound here, and focus upon the possibility of bears. On second sight we realize that we are confronted by a pair of large male coati mundis, monkey-like relatives of the raccoon. Sparring in upright position, they stand more than half as tall as we. Before we can move, they sense our presence, and with excited squeaks they vanish into the scrub bushes. We realize that our responses have been dulled by civilization and are relieved that we have not encountered more formidable adversaries with reflexes quicker than our own.

We move ahead, more alert now, but a bit ashamed at having interrupted some event of nature, a squabble over a bit of hunting territory or a contest for an unseen female. We reflect that modern man is an intruder in the domain of the wild, even when he passes quietly through. As we move down the bed of the rocky gulley, the trail becomes less distinct. We pass a series of small rock-bound basins, each full of water and teeming with a variety of small fishes. Algae and larger water plants are in evidence everywhere. The air is cooler, and the low vegetation is again lush and green. Grotesque, water-carved boulders abound. Rounding the final bend, we behold the big spring, the source of the river.

The Big Spring

We are standing on a sandy beach looking across an acre of water at the tilted layers of limestone which form the surrounding cliffs. In crevices grow a profusion of mosses, ferns, flowering plants, and small trees. A dense forest crowns the top. From the left margin flows the stream, cool, clear, and swift, and lined by green, bushy vegetation. Climbing halfway up the cliff to our right, we are able to view the underwater panorama in crystal clarity. A plomb line informs us that the water is over fifty feet deep; yet every stone is visible, even the dark cave at the foot of the cliff which drains the bowels of the Sierra. In the shallows, where the river spills over the edge of the basin, several schools of fishes remain motionless or peck at bottom algae. Others swim along the sandy shore. Two large mountain mullets emerge from the depths, swim rapidly among the schools at the river's birth, and return to the deep water. A larger fish, perhaps three or four feet long, cruises along the bottom of the basin. Every fish may be identified and counted. The spectacle is breath-taking. Has civilized man ever beheld this sight? Did the aboriginal tribes visit this place before? We reflect that during our entire day's journey, we have not encountered a single trace of man—no rubbish or habitation, nor even a footprint. How long will this paradise remain virgin?

Back down on the beach, lunch is the first order of business. A small fire provides coals to toast the tortillas. After dousing and burying the ashes, we remove chemical analysis equipment from the knapsacks and proceed to analyze water samples from different parts of the basin. Next, a brief refreshing swim. After repacking the knapsacks we begin to retrace our steps toward camp, for it is afternoon, and already the clouds are building up on the crest of the Sierra.

As we pass up the rocky gulley, thinking of the paradise being left behind, we suddenly realize that we are not alone. Stopping abruptly, we scan the forest and pools ahead and gradually make out a magnificent buck deer. He had been drinking, and our attention was alerted when he raised his head. For a silent, motionless moment we gaze at each other, then with an effortless bound he disappears into the trees. The return trip is without further incident except for the sighting of a large cream-and-black rat snake six or seven feet long, a magnificent specimen which we are unable to pursue into the thorny underbrush. The sun has just disappeared behind the clouds ranging the western mountains when we reach camp, and we are surprised to find that we have visitors.

Back at Camp

It has been our practice to pay the native children from the nearby settlement a few centavos for local specimens brought in to us in good, preferably living, condition. This evening several children await our arrival. We hastily get the evening meal started and then begin examining the treasures they have accumulated. One has a pocket full of lizards. Another has two toads and several small frogs of a species which I have been unable to capture. Another has a live snake tied to the end of a strand of twine-like grass. Still another has collected a series of ticks from his father's leg. The last little boy has been sitting there waiting with a large tarantula on a short stick. As the spider walks toward the child's hand, he simply grabs the opposite end of the stick—this has apparently been going on much of the afternoon. Containers are scarce in the jungle.

Eventually all the specimens are purchased, labeled, recorded, and preserved, and we settle down for a moment's rest while we consume the evening meal. We have a strong conscience about killing and preserving living creatures, and we justify our actions on the grounds that some day, when civilization has moved in, whole populations and races of living creatures will be destroyed. In the long run it is perhaps justifiable to sacrifice a few for the permanent museum record of what was really here. As we clean up after supper, it is getting quite dark. In the fading light we are aware of the evening sounds of birds, insects, and bats. The air is thick with bats, mostly insect-feeders, but among them are a few blood-sucking vampires.

It is always interesting to visit the river at night to watch the catfishes, the goby-like fishes, and the large river shrimp (which reach the size of small lobsters). But if the day holds surprises, the night is even more unpredictable. One may occasionally hear an owl or catch sight of a rear-fanged snake, but night is the time of mammals. On previous night expeditions, we have encountered coatis, foxes, jaguarundis, ocelots, armadillos, tlaquaches (opossums), and the giant weasel-like tepechichi (tayra) which is known to run down deer. Tonight we plan to spear fishes in the creek, or arroyo, which enters the river nearby.

With headlights, heavy cloth bags, and a three-pronged gig we set out for the night's adventure. We have scarcely left camp when we stop short to analyze a totally unfamiliar sound, a low continuous groaning noise which rises and falls in slow monotony, louder and louder from out of the dense forest. We finally conclude that this is the breeding chorus of the giant marine toad congregated in some shallow isolated jungle pond resulting from last night's rain. The noise level becomes unbelievable. We are tempted to investigate, but somehow it seems unwise to leave the trail and move back into the jungle on a very dark night. Other hungry spectators may be attracted, and if there is potential danger, it could not be heard over the din of the chorus. It is not necessary to learn all the secrets of the jungle on one trip; so we proceed to the arroyo as originally planned.

Descending the steep banks, we are careful to push back the vegetation ahead, lest we place our feet near a snake. As we step into the water the tree frogs singing on the opposite bank become silent. They are ventriloquists and very difficult to locate, but the native children somehow catch them during the daytime. Slowly wading upstream we note dense stands of grass-like vegetation emerging from the water's edge. Elephant ears and other large-leaved plants line the water's edge, and bamboo thickets growing along the steep banks meet overhead. Here a wolf spider, there a water strider, and in the deeper pools the creatures we have come to collect. For several hours we wade, sometimes up to our armpits, alert to sounds in the forest above, looking out for snakes, caimans, and crocodiles which may be in the area. Spearing is moderately successful, and we return to camp with several large shrimp, two predacious goby-like fishes, and one adult male cichlid fish with the prominent fatty hump on its head.

The toad chorus has ceased. As we wend back toward camp, our lights pick up a pair of golden eyes in the low bushes fifty yards ahead. We approach, but they keep moving silently to the side. This is probably a small fox. Back at camp we preserve the night's catch and wash up at the river's edge. As we finish recording the night's events in the field log book, we become aware of a deep ominous coughing sound. The hunting call of the jaguar. The first impulse is to locate the sound—how close and which direction. We know better, of course. Reverberating through the forest it comes from nowhere—and everywhere. In the still of the jungle night, this is the only sound we hear. The beast is not immediately upon us, and, in any event, we are not likely to be bothered.

Tired, but satisfied with the day's work, we retire to our hammocks. It is nearly midnight, and the birds will awaken us early. The call of the jaguar fades into the night. Rain begins to fall. Drop by drop we hear it at first, then the downpour. The jungle is at peace as it has been, night after night, for eons of time. This is an ancient and beautiful world, a world of balanced harmony. *Each creature has its role in the scheme of things.* How does it all work? How does the living community maintain itself throughout time? How does the soil retain its fertility? How do the cycles of nature go on and on? Sleep.

Two Decades Later

We return twenty years later. Passing down the Pan American highway, we plan to revisit the site where a lone graduate student spent six months studying nature as it is. On the arid land along the highway, formerly covered with scrub vegetation, not a tree may be seen. Cotton fields extend unbroken for miles and miles. Occasionally we pass a group of buildings, a cotton gin, a farm machinery garage, several large pesticide storage tanks. Nearby is a small airstrip with several sprayer planes parked to the side.

With some difficulty we locate the turn-off and are surprised to find that we can now drive all the way to the site of the former sugar mill. Where our jungle once stood, tractors are now plowing the soil in preparation for the spring corn crop. There will be two "plantings." The first will be a broadcast of strychnine-soaked grain to eliminate the doves, grackles, and parrots. The second will be for the new crop. Up on the side of the Sierra, even on the steepest slopes, land is being cleared for new fields. Here and there the remaining patches of forest are being cut, and wisps of gray smoke arise from the burning piles of branches, stumps, and roots.

Leaving the car we walk to the river and note erosion gulleys where none existed before. The native settlement has grown to a village. There is a one-room school without toilet facilities. A few bushes have been left out back on the river bank. The river itself is lower than we have ever seen it, and the stream bears an unhealthy odor. It is turbid and still, for upstream dams and diversionary ditches carry water to the fields for irrigation. The sounds are those of civilization, people, tractors, trucks climbing the steep grade of the Sierra to the lumber mill above.

As we drive slowly away, we realize that we have experienced a vanished world and that we must set down in print what we have seen and what we have experienced so that a new generation of students will understand how it all got this way. *Theirs will be the task of correcting the mistakes and excesses of our generation.*

1. ecology
and the
individual

. . . In treating physiological phenomena, assimilation,
respiration, growth, and the like, which have a varying
magnitude under varying external conditions of
temperature, light, supply of materials, &c., it is customary
to speak of three cardinal points, the minimal condition
below which the phenomenon ceases altogether, the optimal
condition at which it is exhibited to its highest observed
degree, and the maximal condition above which
it ceases again . . .
F. F. Blackman 1905.

Introduction

Miscellaneous observations about the lives and habits of plants and animals have long been part of man's knowledge, and collectively they constitute the field of *natural history*. Observations concerning growing seasons, breeding habits, food habits, and behavior patterns fall into this category. The formal field of ecology has developed from the accumulated natural-history wisdom of the ages, but ecology is more than natural history.

Ecology seeks to describe nature in quantitative terms. Ecology is based upon numerical observations; it deals with ratios; and it is intimately concerned with rates at which natural processes occur. For many years ecology was known as quantitative natural history, but the field of ecology has additional parameters.

Quantitative information has led to the development of ideas about total functional systems of nature, and the natural history information has now been organized into a set of formal principles which govern the behavior of the natural systems. In some cases the principles can be expressed mathematically as differential equations. In other cases we still have to use words or, at best, mathematical approximations. Ecology is a field which is still growing and developing, but it represents man's best attempt to understand the living world. Its message cannot be ignored by any intelligent citizen, least of all by those citizens who through administrative, political, religious, or social position can influence the patterns by which groups of humans relate to the natural system.

Biological Systems

Before proceeding to discuss the principles of ecology, as we currently understand them, it is necessary to say a few words about the biological systems themselves. Life is organized according to certain functional patterns which have been worked out by trial-and-error processes through the generations of time. Considering the fact that life has been on this earth at least 3 billion years (and that is a great many hours and minutes), and considering the fact that many billions of trial-and-error experiments are in progress throughout the world at any one particular moment, it is understandable that complex and workable life patterns have come into existence and that such patterns have themselves become organized into yet more complex entities. The functional systems of nature are thus arranged in a hierarchy of patterns from relatively simple to relatively complex. The functional systems of a given level of organization become the components of the next higher level. Certain laws or principles govern the operation of all biological systems, but as we shall see, at each level some generalizations and principles become evident which are unique to that particular level.

The levels of biological organization are illustrated in Figure 1.1. The individual organism is composed of organ systems which are, in turn, made up of organs, these of tissues, and so on. Approached from the other direction, *individual organisms* (oak trees, zebras, sea gulls, etc.) make up single-species groups called *populations* (groves, herds, flocks, etc.). These live and interact with populations of other species and together constitute natural *communities* (forest, grassland, marine, etc.). A given community together with the environment with which it is normally associated makes up an *ecosystem* (forest, grassland, marine, etc.). All the ecosystems of the world considered as a collec-

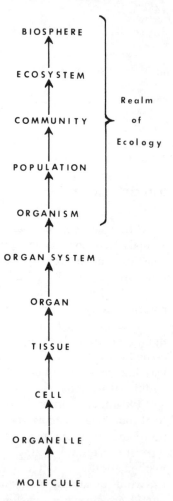

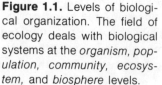

Figure 1.1. Levels of biological organization. The field of ecology deals with biological systems at the *organism, population, community, ecosystem,* and *biosphere* levels.

tive unit comprise the *biosphere*. The field of ecology embraces those levels of organization from the *individual* through the *biosphere*. The composition and relationships of these levels will be discussed in subsequent chapters.

A biological system is a living unit of any size or degree of complexity which has a structural and functional integrity. It may be a cell or an ecosystem. Since it is a living unit, it displays certain properties which, taken together, distinguish it from all nonliving systems:

It embodies a recognizable structure.

It carries out orderly functional processes.

It undergoes a regular pattern of development and maturation.

It reproduces itself more or less exactly.

It is capable of long-range, orderly genetic change.

It survives only within a certain prescribed range of environmental conditions.

It maintains its integrity in the face of a hostile environment.

Its structure and function are finely adjusted to operate under the environmental conditions to which it is normally subjected.

It possesses internal regulatory mechanisms which permit it to offset or to recover from the effects of moderate deviations from the usual environmental conditions.

It cannot cope with severe deviations from the usual conditions. These result in permanent damage or death.

Although generally characteristic of all living systems, these principles vary in detail when applied to different systems of a given level and especially when applied to systems of different levels of biological organization.

The Individual as an Ecological System

The smallest ecological unit is the *individual organism*. Except in the case of rare identical twins and individuals arising by certain asexual processes, all organisms are genetically unique. As a result, even closely related organisms differ in form, function, and ability to adjust or respond to conditions of the environment. Closely related organisms, though differing in some genes, share much of their genetic material in common. Hence, the small differences observed within a given group of organisms may be thought of as variation around a single theme. As we shall see later, this small variability, arising from gene mutation and recombination, is of great importance in permitting survival in the face of a variable environment.

During its life history, the individual passes through a regular series of events, beginning with fertilization, passing through a sequence of developmental stages to maturity, and followed by a period of senescence and death. At each stage the form and function are characteristic for that life period.

The flow of chemicals and energy—Throughout its life each individual must obtain from the environment (or from stored food reserves) certain necessities. These include *inorganic substances* (water, nitrogen, sodium, potassium, calcium, magnesium, iron, etc.) as well as specific *organic chemicals* (carbohydrates, lipids, amino acids, and vitamins) for use as building blocks and chemical factories. In addition, every living organism must constantly derive from the environment a quantity of *energy* sufficient to support the various metabolic processes of the body. This energy is universally derived by chemical oxidation (i.e., burning) of organic compounds. All animals and some plants take in both fuel (organic compounds) and oxygen to provide the needed energy. Green plants, however, manufacture their own energy-rich fuel from carbon dioxide, water, and sunlight by a process known as *photosynthesis*. Since oxygen is a by-product of photosynthesis, the green plants even produce a portion of the oxygen which they need to burn the fuel. The end products of oxidation are carbon dioxide and water (and nitrates, phosphates, and sulfates if certain proteins and lipids are oxidized). A few species of bacteria and blue-green algae have developed the ability to oxidize organic compounds in the absence of oxygen. These species may employ iron, sulfur, and other elements as hydrogen acceptors in place of oxygen. These general processes are illustrated in Figure 1.2.

As a result of its metabolic processes, every organism discards or *excretes* into the environment certain by-products or wastes. If oxidation has been complete, the organism will discharge the chemicals, carbon dioxide, water, nitrates, phosphates, and sulfates. Generally the oxidation is not complete, however, and many organisms also release urea, uric acids, other organic acids, ammonia, etc. Some bacteria and blue-green algae may release methane and hydrogen sulfide gases, as well as nitrites, sulfites, etc. Regardless of whether oxidation is complete or incomplete, all organisms release into the environment large quantities of "waste energy" in the form of heat.

Every living organism also releases into the environment certain chemical substances which are not "waste" in the usual low-energy sense, but they are high-energy organic compounds which seem to have important functional roles and which may be thought of as bodily *secretions*. These include such chemicals as antibiotics, mucus, and special odiferous substances, as well as certain organized structures such as skin cells, shed exoskeletons, feathers, hair, and gametes.

From the foregoing discussion we may derive the following important ecological principle. *Every living organism modifies its environment by the removal*

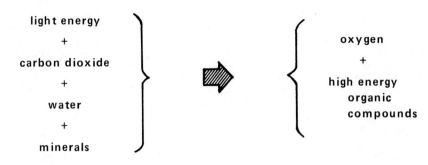

PHOTOSYNTHESIS

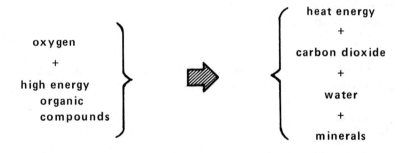

RESPIRATION

Figure 1.2. The buildup and breakdown of organic material through the reciprocal processes of photosynthesis and respiration.

of certain substances and through the addition of others. Different kinds of organisms do different things and at different rates, of course, but all modify their environments in one way or another. This means that all organisms influence the environments of their neighbors. This is a cardinal point in ecology. It leads to success or failure when organisms attempt to live side by side. This principle is illustrated in Figure 1.3.

Figure 1.3. Modification of the environment by the individual organism. The individual removes certain types of chemicals and energy from the environment, changes their states, and returns them to the environment as wastes and secretions.

Maintenance of Life in the Hostile Environment

Every living organism must maintain its chemical and physical integrity if it is to survive. To accomplish this the organism must selectively remove from the environment what it needs, selectively eliminate that which is no longer useful, and carry out these processes in spite of an ever-changing environment. The maintenance of a constant internal integrity entails a variety of adjustment and regulatory processes which collectively keep the system in a steady state equilibrium with its environment. This phenomenon, known as *homeostasis*, is one of the most remarkable features of living systems, and it is especially conspicuous at the level of the individual.

Consider the oyster, exposed to the air at low tide and submerged when the tide is in, subjected to fresh water after rainfall and salt water when there is no rain. It must endure summer heat and winter cold, the heavy silts of spring floods and the clear water of summer. Through it all the oyster must survive, grow, and reproduce its kind. This tenacity of life, the ability to keep going in spite of environmental change, is displayed to greater or lesser degree by all living organisms.

For each life history stage of an organism there is an optimum set of environmental conditions. So long as these conditions are met, the organism will grow, develop, and function in normal fashion. If one or more of the environmental factors deviates significantly from the normal range, then the organism is placed under stress. The stress condition may be sharp and sudden, or it may be low level and of long duration. It may be characterized by either an excess or a deficiency of a given environmental factor. In any case the organism must respond by some means which will aid in offsetting the effect of the stress agent.

Response to environmental stress—Individuals possess a remarkable portfolio of response mechanisms for dealing with environmental stress. Some simply move away to more favorable areas. Others become physiologically inactive and wait out the unfavorable period in a dormant or semidormant state. Others stay and tolerate certain internal body conditions which faithfully follow those of the external environment. All living organisms, however, show some ability to *regulate* the internal environment, and the ability to regulate is greatest among the higher forms of life.

Among those organisms which remain active, one of the first measurable signs of stress is the elevated requirement for oxygen. Respiration increases, but since the respiratory apparatus itself poses certain limitations, a smaller fraction of the organism's bodily resources remains available for normal metabolic activity when it is under stress. Thus, the organism is subjected to a *metabolic load* in proportion to the degree and duration of the stress factor.

To counteract the stress situation the organism must reorder the metabolic programs of the body. This often involves increased production of certain hormones and enzymes accompanied by the decreased production or inhibition of others. Certain metabolic pathways become favored over others. Body fluid concentrations are altered. Excretory products may be accumulated or voided in unmetabolized form. Long-continued stress may result in the harmful depletion of certain chemical and energy reserves, accumulation of salt deposits, hypertrophy of certain tissues and organs, atrophy of others, exhaustion of hormonal and enzyme capabilities, inhibition of reproduction, altered behavior patterns, and eventually death.

To protect the body from the potentially dangerous effects of stress most organisms have developed the ability to *acclimate.* This involves a series of metabolic readjustments which permit continued function with minimal deleterious effect in the face of long-enduring, low-level stress situations. A persistent high noise level can be "tuned out" and eventually ignored so long as the intensity remains reasonably constant. An environmental temperature increase can be tolerated much more readily if the temperature rise is sufficiently gradual to permit the high temperature adaptive enzymes to come into play. Organisms can adjust so long as the extremes are not too great and the rate of change is not too rapid. Acclimation thus permits the organism to carry on nearly normal bodily functions over a fairly wide range of environmental conditions, even into the stress zones.

It was pointed out above that stress may be occasioned by either the excess or deficiency of a given environmental factor. This concept may be generalized to the level of an ecological principle. *With respect to the factors of the environment, life is adjusted to some intermediate condition.* For each type of organism and for each stage of its development, there is a limited *range of tolerance* within which life is possible. Somewhere within this total range of tolerance, there is an optimal zone or *range of normal activity.* Both above and below this optimal range and continuing to the limits of tolerance there are *zones of stress* wherein the organism either cannot carry on normal activity or in which body functions are impaired. These features are illustrated in Figure 1.4.

With respect to temperature, for example, it may be too hot or too

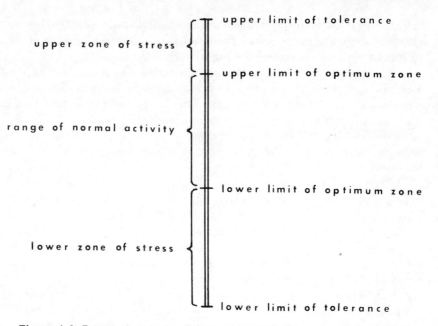

Figure 1.4. Range of a single environmental factor (such as temperature) in relation to the organism's normal activity, zones of stress, and limits of tolerance.

cold. With respect to iodine, this element may be present in poisonous quantity or it may be so scarce as to result in deficiency symptoms. Requirements and tolerances vary from one species to another, but all have become adjusted to the general conditions of life in which the organism normally dwells. Those individuals which fail to adjust to their environments perish without leaving progeny. It is generally true that immature forms of a species (eggs, larvae, babies, etc.) are the stages least tolerant of environmental stress, and it is here that the highest rates of environmentally induced mortality occur.

All natural environments are capricious. They involve many factors acting together, and although the nature of the variation is to some extent predictable, unusual extremes do occur. Therefore, some degree of stress is a regular feature of existence of organisms in all environments. Environmental selection for the strong and the adaptable has been the overriding consideration throughout the history of life on this planet. It has been the primary sieve through which new genetic material has been strained, the anvil of adaptive evolution.

Earlier in this chapter it was pointed out that no two individuals are exactly alike, and the evolutionary significance of this fact now becomes clear. Since the environment varies from place to place and from time to time, it is of definite advantage to a species that its members possess a certain amount of variety in ranges of tolerance, zones of optimum, and so on. Thus, the group has greater potential than the individual, and group survival is insured in spite of individual hardships which are inevitable.

Suggestions for Further Reading

BLACKMAN, F. F. "Optima and Limiting Factors." *Ann. of Bot.* 19 1905.
BORRADAILE, L. A. *The Animal and its Environment.* London: Oxford University Press, 1923.
BUCHSBAUM, R., and BUCHSBAUM M. *Basic Ecology.* Pittsburgh: Boxwood Press, 1958.
BURNETT, A. L., and EISNER T. *Animal Adaptation.* New York: Holt, Rinehart, and Winston, 1964.
DARNELL, R. M. *Organism and Environment: A Manual of Quantitative Ecology.* W. H. Freeman & Co., 1971.
DAUBENMIRE, R. F. *Plants and Environment: A Textbook of Autecology.* New York: John C. Wiley & Sons, 1959.
FARB, P., and the editors of *Life. Ecology.* Life Nature Library. New York: Time Inc., 1963.
ODUM, E. P., *Ecology.* New York: Holt, Rinehart, and Winston, 1963.

2. the environment

> The environment is a complex of many factors, each
> dependent upon another, or upon several others, in such a
> way that a change in any one effects changes in one or
> more others. The most important environmental factors are
> water, atmospheric moisture, light, temperature, pressure,
> oxygen, carbon dioxide, nitrogen, food, enemies, materials
> used in abodes, etc. In nature the combinations of these in
> proportions requisite for the abode of a considerable number
> of animals are called "environmental complexes."
>
> Victor E. Shelford, 1913

Introduction

We have seen that the individual organism is adapted to some middle range of environmental conditions and that normal function becomes more difficult as conditions of the environment approach the limits of tolerance. In the present chapter we shall examine the environment in greater detail, but the reference point is always the organism. To the ecologist the environment in itself is of no particular interest except as it relates to the living systems.

Factors Controlling the Distribution of Organisms in Nature

With respect to a given environmental factor, different organisms exhibit different ranges of tolerance. Some have wide ranges, others show narrow ranges. Some do better at the upper end of the spectrum, others are more successful at the low end. A convenient set of terminology has been developed to describe the relative tolerance ranges of organisms (Figure 2.1), and experimental studies permit the ranges of many species to be given in quantitative terms.

The environment consists of many factors, and for each factor the organism displays a characteristic range of tolerance. For example, the tolerance range may be wide for temperature and narrow for moisture. Since, however, the factors do act in combination the available level of one factor may greatly influence the organism's ability to withstand extremes of another. Certain higher plants are able to tolerate drought conditions better

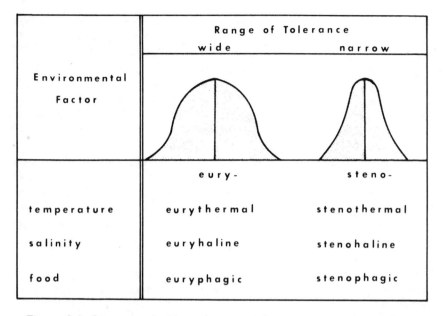

Figure 2.1. Concepts of wide and narrow tolerance ranges of organisms as illustrated by three environmental factors.

if the weather remains cool and if the soil nitrogen is not critically low. In hot weather most mammals maintain moderate body temperatures through the cooling effects of evaporative water loss. Access to an ample supply of drinking water is thus essential to their prolonged survival in extreme heat.

Within a given species, not all the individuals show exactly the same limits of tolerance. The geographic range of the common leopard frog extends throughout eastern North America from Canada to Central America. Canadian frogs tolerate low temperatures, but not high temperatures. For the Central American frogs, the reverse is true. Each is adapted to survive under conditions of the environment in which it normally lives.

The ability to adapt, however, has its limits. In the cold, treeless tundra of northern Canada one encounters no leopard frogs; indeed, no frogs at all, nor any other amphibian. The environment is simply too harsh for amphibians or trees. *The ability of an organism to survive in a given environment clearly depends upon two conditions: the nature and variability of the factors making up the particular environment and the position of the organism's tolerance limits.* This important principle aids in explaining the patterns of distribution of plants and animals around the world.

Organisms do not survive under conditions for which they are not adapted, but neither do they inhabit all the areas where environmental conditions lie within their ranges of physiological tolerance. The American cactus family is not represented in the vast desert areas of north Africa, and the sea lamprey is not native to Lake Michigan, even though in retrospect, we know that conditions favorable to its survival were present. In both cases inability to get there was the problem.

Even if transportation is afforded, however, many organisms are prevented from occupying otherwise favorable environments by the presence of certain other species. Restriction in this case is brought about by some type of *biological interaction*. In many cases the interaction is *indirect* and is mediated through the nonliving environment. Elimination of the tree canopy in the deciduous forests of eastern North America is almost invariably followed by invasion of grasses and shrubs previously held in check by reduced light conditions prevailing at the forest floor. In other instances the interaction is *direct,* involving either physical contact or direct communication between the interacting organisms. Parasitism, predation, disease, antibiotic inhibition, and similar phenomena fall into this category. Eradication of predators, for example, is almost sure to result in a spread of prey individuals into more exposed areas from which they were previously excluded.

In many cases the physical or nonliving factors (abiotic factors) *of the environment set the absolute limits of a given organism's distribution in nature, but the biological factors* (biotic factors) *determine which portion of this potential area is actually occupied.* This is not the whole story, however. *In other cases biological factors permit the occupation of an area from which an organism would otherwise have been excluded.* The forest canopy modifies the environment of the forest floor so that mosses, ferns, violets, and a host of shade-tolerant and moisture-sensitive plants can flourish. In the deserts of the American southwest, the tall saguaro cactus provides ideal nesting sites for the Gila woodpecker, which can drill into the cactus. Abandoned woodpecker holes, in turn, are eventually occupied by elf owls and a variety of other desert birds which are unable to drill holes for themselves. Both principles are important in explaining the distribution patterns of organisms in nature.

The Habitat

The place where an organism dwells is called its *habitat,* a term which connotes both geographic and environmental information. The habitat of the sailfin molly (a popular aquarium fish) is the shallow coastal marshes, lagoons, and small streams of the Gulf coast and south Atlantic states. The species favors brackish (partly salty) waters with relatively dense aquatic vegetation, muddy bottoms, and no current, although it sometimes occurs naturally in fresh waters with slow to moderate current flow. In describing the habitat of the sailfin molly, a distinction has been made between the *primary habitat,* where the species seems to flourish best (and is most abundant), and the *secondary habitat,* where it is occasionally present (generally, in lower concentration). Primary and secondary habitat are often referred to as *optimal* and *suboptimal* habitat. During the most productive seasons and during moderate years, organisms often move out and occupy the various areas of suboptimal habitat, but during times of severe environmental conditions, the individuals become restricted to the areas of optimal habitat.

In the habitat description given above, only the salient features have been given. No effort has been made to list all the physical, chemical, and biological factors, and the factors listed are not given in quantitative terms. To do so would be a complex and lengthy, if not impossible, task, and no complete habitat description has ever been presented for any species. In any given habitat, however, certain features stand out as being of especial importance, and the experienced ecologist quickly learns to recognize the *significant environmental variables* operative in a particular situation. For primitive man, who lived close to nature, this ability often spelled survival in unbelievably hostile environments, as field anthropologists have repeatedly testified.

Individual vs. Group Factors

There are two general ways of viewing the environment, both of which are important. In the first place, it may be considered in terms of the *individual factors* as they act independently or as they act in combination with one or two other factors of the environment. These individual factors include *physical factors* (temperature, light, moisture, pressure, current, gravity, etc.) and *chemical factors* (oxygen, carbon dioxide, sodium, potassium, iodine, bromine, etc.). A great deal of experimental work has been carried out on the effects of individual factors on metabolism, activities, and survival of organisms, and advanced ecological works often treat the individual factors in great detail.

On the other hand, the environment may be considered in terms of *groups of factors* acting collectively. In this view all the atmospheric factors might be considered together as the "weather factor"; similarly, chemical and physical properties of the substratum would be considered as the "soil factor." Biological factors invariably fall into this group category because it is impossible for one organism to affect another in only a single way. It is relatively easy to set up experiments dealing with group factors, but it is exceedingly difficult to arrive at precise interpretations of the resulting data due to the variety of factors which are varying simultaneously and because many of the factors may be unknown or at least unmeasured. Group-factor experiments, like many field observations, represent correlations or approximations, but they are nonetheless valuable and are sometimes the only types of information available concerning the infinitely complex systems of nature.

Regularity and Irregularity of Environmental Factor Variation

As pointed out earlier, the environment is made up of a great many factors, each of which tends to vary. The pattern of variability is not random, however, but is fairly regular. On land it is associated primarily with the day-night and seasonal cycles of weather patterns. In marine coastal environments, it is also associated with the tidal cycle. Nights tend to be cooler, darker, and more humid than days. Winters have shorter days, less light, and colder weather than do summers. High tides flood more beach and are accompanied by stronger water currents than low tides when desiccation becomes a problem. *Spring tides* (biweekly high, high tides) exhibit exaggerated tidal effects in contrast with the *neap tides* (biweekly low, low tides).

In organisms which have long associated with a particular type of physical environment, the breeding, feeding, and activity patterns have become evolutionarily adjusted so that they are timed in relation to the cyclic environmental features. Therefore, the biological factors of the environment likewise show patterns of rhythmic intensity (Figure 2.2). In many instances the biological activities take place in direct response to specific environmental factors which act as signals or cues. The cock crows at the first rays of dawn. The jaguar hunts at night. Migratory birds head north in response to increased day length. Toads breed in response to the first heavy rain of the season. It often occurs that the biological rhythm develops a genetic basis so that even when the organisms are maintained in a relatively constant environment in the laboratory, isolated from all obvious environmental signals, the rhythm persists. Sometimes the "biological clocks" can be readjusted to a new set of environmental signals, but in other cases the clocks are set at birth and can be readjusted only with great difficulty, if at all.

Despite the regularity of daily and seasonal environmental patterns, occasional extreme irregularities do occur, often with catastrophic biological results. Such irregularities may be of either local or widespread occurrence. Earthquakes, tornadoes, severe storms, floods, forest fires, and the like may have relatively local effects. Drought, hard winter, unseasonal cold snaps, and so on tend to be more regional. Organisms cannot genetically anticipate the unusual extreme, so in either case severe hardship and mass mortality may result. Local damage is often easily repaired by organisms which move in from adjacent areas, but regional damage may take many years because of the distance which must be traversed by all the various species necessary for repopulation and repair.

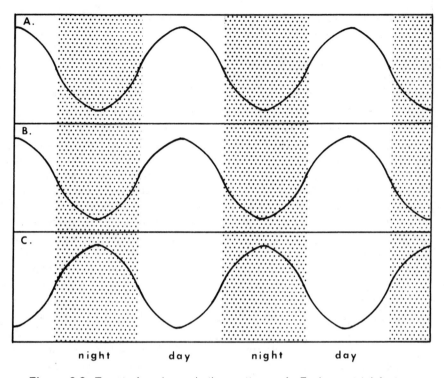

night   day   night   day

Figure 2.2. Twenty-four hour rhythm patterns. A. Environmental factors, such as light and temperature. B. Activity pattern of a diurnal (= day-active) organism. C. Activity pattern of a nocturnal (= night-active) organism.

Environmental Classification

Many systems have been developed for classifying natural environments. Some systems are based upon climatic factors, others upon soils. Some take into account the vegetation, others the animal life. In spite of this seeming diversity, most systems do not vary a great deal from one another because the distribution of vegetation, soils, and animals all depend initially upon the climate of the area. Accordingly, they are all correlated with one another. The climate, in turn, depends primarily upon global factors (earth's rotation, seasonal tilting of the earth's axis, position of major land and water masses, etc.). To illustrate the correlations, as a general rule of thumb, it may be stated that:

The climate of an area determines the plants which can live in the area.
The climate and the plants determine the characteristics of the soil.

The climate, plants, and soil together tend to determine the patterns of animal distribution.

These rules are clearly oversimplifications of the situation, as many exceptions are known, but the statements are generally true and will be quite useful in attempting to visualize the patterns of nature on a broad scope. Let us now examine these statements in greater detail.

Climate—Air is a remarkable constant mixture of gases which, in the dry state, includes about 78 percent nitrogen, 21 percent oxygen, and small amounts of other gases (carbon dioxide, argon, hydrogen, neon, helium). Suspended in the air are variable amounts of moisture and fine particles of organic and inorganic matter which may collectively be called "dust." As the earth rotates, the air tends to lag behind, the greatest lag occurring in the equatorial belt where the surface is rotating fastest. Due to solar heating, the tropical air expands, rises, and moves toward the poles. There it cools, descends to the surface, and heads back toward the equator. This is the basic generating system that keeps air in constant motion with respect to the earth's surface. Many other factors enter the picture to determine the complicated details of the world pattern of surface air circulation. Of especial importance is the fact that the patterns tend to change in response to the seasonal shift in the earth's axis of rotation.

Long-range average patterns of atmospheric conditions are referred to as the *climate* of a region; their day-to-day occurrence is called the *weather.* Climate includes the annual quantity and seasonal distribution of temperature, light, precipitation, and humidity. These factors are determined by position on the earth's surface, overall atmospheric circulation patterns, and neighboring features, such as position of mountain ranges, large water bodies, and land masses.

From the biological standpoint, the most meaningful way of describing the climate of an area is on the basis of the *moisture factor.* This is defined by the quantity and seasonal distribution of precipitation and by the potential for water loss (through evaporation and transpiration by plants). *Evapotranspiration,* in turn, reflects the prevailing temperature, saturation deficit of the air, and air movement. Distribution of the major climatic zones of North America, based largely upon the moisture factor, is given in Figure 2.3.

Soil — Soil is a relatively dense medium which serves to anchor and nourish larger plants and to provide support for the myriads of microbes and small animals which comprise the soil microflora and microfauna. In texture, soil is made up of particles of many sizes including both mineral (sand, clay, and silt) and organic materials. Between the particles are located pore spaces which, in saturated soils, may be filled with water. In unsaturated soils these spaces may be filled largely with air. Since plant roots

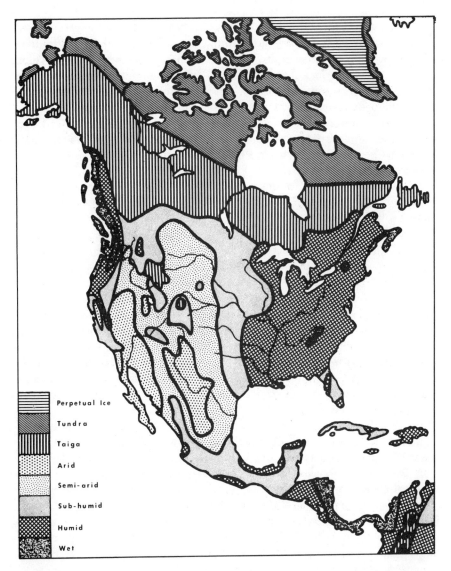

Figure 2.3. Climatic zones of North America. All the principal climatic types of the world are represented. Note the diversity of climatic types of the United States alone. (Adapted from *Climate and Man*, 1941 Yearbook of Agriculture.)

need air, the degree of saturation of the soil is very important in determining local patterns of plant distribution.

Among the inorganic constituents of soils, the most abundant chemical elements are oxygen, silicon, aluminum, iron, calcium, sodium, potassium, and magnesium. A great many types of minerals are present in smaller quantity, however, and it is these trace-amount minerals which, for the most part, act as minimal-quantity limiting factors in relation to plant distribution. In some areas of the world, especially in certain low, arid evaporation basins (California desert basins, Great Salt Lake basin, and Dead Sea basin), the mineral content of the soil may become so high that the soil is said to be salty. In such soil, plant distribution may be restricted by an excess of soil minerals.

The organic content of soils varies greatly from one soil type to another. In certain bog soils, it may constitute over 99 percent of the dry weight of the soil, whereas in certain desert areas, it may make up less than 1 percent. The chemical and physical properties of the soil depend largely upon the nature and quantity of the organic matter present, and this, in turn, depends upon the types of vegetation from which it was derived.

Natural, undisturbed soils house myriads of small organisms including primarily bacteria, fungi, protozoa, worms, mites, and small insects. These forms burrow through the soil and aid in maintaining its porosity. Their most important function, however, is the breakdown or decomposition of the organic material which falls to the soil surface. Only after the decomposition process is completed can the minerals be reutilized by the larger plants. In natural soils these organisms may exist in concentrations of nearly a million per square meter of soil surface. Because of the nature to their activities and their abundance, these organisms are absolutely critical to the normal functioning of the systems of nature. Any factor or combination of factors that reduce their abundance, diversity, or ability to function must leave certain waste-disposal jobs undone. The cycles of a balanced system thus become unbalanced, and certain wastes accumulate.

Rain falling on the soil surface percolates down through the pore spaces of the soil, dissolving minerals and other soluble materials along the way. Plant roots remove some of the water, and they selectively remove certain minerals as they are needed. The water, in turn, is transported up through the tissues of the plants, and it may be lost by the process of leaf transpiration.

Soil cross sections reveal recognizable layers or horizons which are characteristic for the vegetational communities which manufacture the soils (see Figure 2.4). For example, prairie soils are deep, black, and highly organic. Soils of the northern coniferous forests are highly stratified with a thin, dark organic layer only at the surface, a whitish layer somewhat deeper,

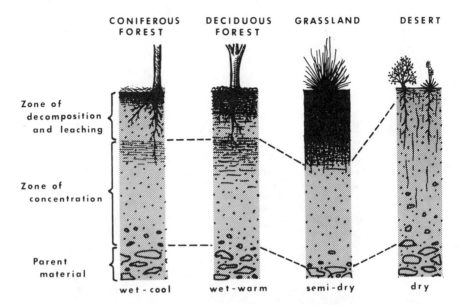

Figure 2.4. The four most important soil types of North America. Cool, moist climates favor the growth of coniferous forests which produce *podzols.* Needles fall to the ground surface, and during the process of decomposition they produce a variety of organic acids. Acidified rainwater percolates downward through the soil removing most of the organic matter and soluble minerals, depositing them several feet below the surface in the zone of concentration. The remaining surface layer is composed primarily of silica and a few other highly insoluble minerals. Warm wet weather favors the growth of deciduous forests which produce *latosols.* Leaves which fall to the surface undergo rapid decomposition but tend to remain fairly alkaline. If the rainfall is only moderate, much of the organic matter and alkaline minerals remain in surface layers, giving them a dark brownish color. Where the rainfall is heavy the large volume of water quickly leaches soluble materials from the surface layers leaving the iron oxides and certain other insoluble minerals which give the surface soils a reddish to yellowish-brown appearance. In semi-arid grasslands the roots penetrate deep in search of water and often die in place leaving organic matter throughout the upper layers of soil. Such black loams or *chernozems* are very fertile. Deserts are characterized by low rainfall and high rates of evaporation. The few plants which manage to grow tend to have deep root systems which die in place. Since little moisture percolates downward through the soil stratification is seldom evident. (Adapted from *Climate and Man,* 1941 Yearbook of Agriculture; *Soil,* 1957 Yearbook of Agriculture; and Kellogg, 1948.)

followed by a characteristic reddish layer below that. Brown forest soils
are intermediate between these two extremes. The distribution of soil types
in North America is given in Figure 2.5. This figure should be compared
with Figure 2.3 showing the distribution of climatic zones in North America.

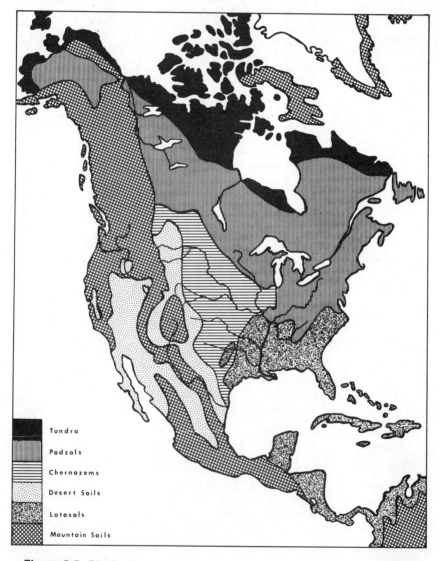

Figure 2.5. Distribution of soil types of North America. All the principal
soil types of the world are represented. Note the close correspondence
of soil types with the climatic zones given in Figure 2.3. (Adapted from
Soil, 1957 Yearbook of Agriculture.)

Suggestions for Further Reading

CHAPMAN, R. N. *Animal Ecology—With Especial Reference to Insects.* New York: McGraw-Hill Book Co., 1931.

HAMBRIDGE, G. *Climate and Man.* Washington, D.C.: U.S. Department of Agriculture (Yearbook), 1941.

HENDERSON, L. J. *The Fitness of the Environment.* Boston: Beacon Press, 1958.

KELLOGG, C. E. "Modern Soil Science." *American Scientist,* vol. 36, 1948.

KNIGHT, C. B. *Basic Concepts of Ecology.* New York: MacMillan Co., 1965.

KORMANDY, E. J. *Concepts of Ecology.* Englewood Cliffs, N. J.: Prentice-Hall, Inc., 1969.

LEHR, P. E.; BURNETT, R. W.; and ZIM, H. S. *Weather—A Guide to Phenomena and Forecasts.* New York: Golden Press, 1957.

PEARSE, A. S. *Animal Ecology.* New York: McGraw-Hill Book Co., 1939.

SHELFORD, V. E. *Animal Communities in Temperate America.* Chicago: University of Chicago Press, 1913.

STEFFERUD, A. *Soil.* Washington, D.C.: U.S. Department of Agriculture (Yearbook), 1957.

WEAVER, J. E., and CLEMENTS, F. E., *Plant Ecology.* New York: McGraw-Hill Book Co., 1938.

3. the

population

Population, when unchecked, increases in a geometrical ratio. Subsistence increases only in an arithmetical ratio. A slight acquaintance with numbers will shew the immensity of the first power in comparison of the second.
Thomas Robert Malthus, 1798.

Population Variability

All organisms of a given "kind" constitute a species. Every member of the species is potentially capable of breeding with all other members of the same species, but members of different species normally cannot interbreed. Each species thus represents a certain array of hereditary material *(gene pool)* which gets reshuffled at each generation and which is distinct from the genetic arrays of other species.

Sharing a common pool of hereditary material all members of the species tend to be superficially alike, but they are not identical. Every species in nature is composed of smaller units called populations. Each population tends to inhabit a unit of more or less optimal habitat, and each population unit is somewhat isolated from other populations by regions of suboptimal habitat. Since individual organisms often find their way from one population to another, the populations may maintain a certain degree of genetic contact with one another. The amount of contact will vary in relation to the nature of the separating barriers and to the fluctuating environmental conditions. Regardless of the genetic exchange from the outside, however, the population is the closest breeding unit in nature (Figure 3.1).

Even within a given population, the individual organisms vary in genetic constitution, and hence, in their appearance, tolerance ranges, and other attributes. But the structure and functional characteristics of the individuals and even the range of variability within each population is closely adjusted to the peculiar conditions of the particular "island" of optimal habitat. Since the patterns of environmental conditions of the various habitat islands

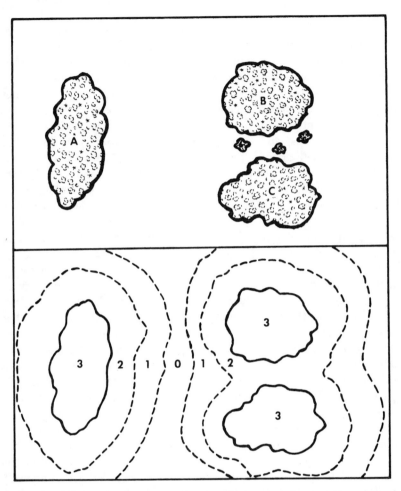

Figure 3.1. Distribution of three hypothetical populations of a woodland snail in relation to optimal and suboptimal habitats. A. Map of vegetation types. Three woodland plots in low wet areas are surrounded by grassland. Plot *a* is separated from the other two by a high dry ridge, but only a low moist ridge separates plots *b* and *c*. B. Theoretical distribution of favorable and unfavorable snail habitat, the highest value indicating the most optimal conditions. Although largely limited to the woods, the snails may sometimes cross the moderate barrier between *b* and *c,* especially in very wet seasons. They almost never cross the major barrier which isolates plot *a*. This means that the populations in plots *b* and *c* maintain genetic contact and thus tend to remain genetically similar over a long period of time. The population in plot *a*, however, is genetically isolated from the other two. Through the accumulation of unshared genetic mutations this population will diverge, and over a long period of time it may become a distinct species.

differ, the average genetic constitution and the range of genetic material available will vary from one population to another.

Two sources of variability within the species are thus recognized: variability *within* each population and variability *between* the different populations. If one has seen a redwood or a human being, he has seen them all only in the most superficial sense. Genetic diversity is critically important in that it endows populations with greater tolerance limits than those possessed by individuals, and the species, in turn, with greater limits than those displayed by the populations. This flexibility enhances species survival in changing environments, often in the face of unforeseen catastrophic environmental events. As will be seen later, the stability of individual populations and species contributes in great measure to the stability of the multi-species systems of nature.

If a population invades a new area where the normal environmental pressures are relaxed, the population tends to spread out, ecologically speaking, and to occupy not only the optimal but all sorts of suboptimal habitats. Such habitat expansion has repeatedly been demonstrated in the case of island-hopping birds, lizards, and insects, in the Pacific archipelagos and the islands of the West Indies. This also tends to occur in mainland populations when a severe environmental restriction is relaxed (elimination of a predator or competing species, for example) or when a new area is invaded. The underlying cause of habitat expansion is clear. Saturation of primary habitat leads to increased competition among members of a given species. This forces some individuals to occupy peripheral habitat (to which they may later become well adapted if the situation continues to prevail). If the peripheral habitat is already occupied by a well-adapted competing species, however, the habitat expansion will not occur. *The degree of genetic and ecological variability of a species, therefore, reflects primarily the balance of two forces:* intraspecific *competition (which leads to expansion) and* interspecific *competition (which leads to restriction).* These forces are illustrated in Figure 3.2.

Certain other factors also influence population variability. These include the total size of the population, degree of genetic contact with other populations, variability of the environment, genetic diversity of the immigrants which initiated the new population, and age of the population. In considering population variability, however, one factor stands out as being of prime importance. Since the variability depends upon a balance of opposing pressures, the nature and degree of the variability tend to change from time to time in response to shifts in the relative strengths of the opposing forces. In a variable environment, such shifts are inevitable.

Numerical Attributes of Populations

We have seen above that populations exhibit a certain amount of *variability* and that they are subject to *environmental pressures* to which they

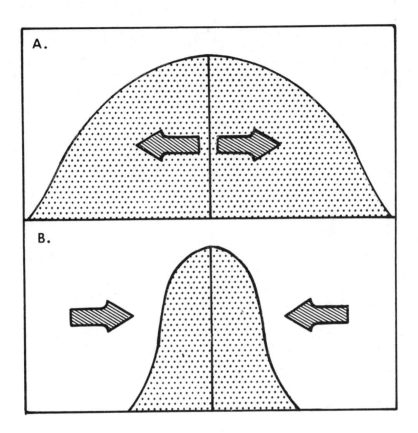

Population variability

Figure 3.2. Effects of intraspecific and interspecific competition. A. Intraspecific competition invariably exerts a pressure for the population to diversify and broaden its utilization of environmental resources. In a complex environment this means that the structural and functional characteristics of the individuals making up the population will tend to become quite variable. B. Interspecific competition occurs when populations of different species vie for the same scarce environmental resources. The pressure in this case is for a given population to specialize in the use of resources for which competition is least. Coexistence may be achieved by specialization. This tends to reduce individual variability within the population. Thus the variability observed in any natural population at a given time will be a reflection of these two opposing pressures.

respond by *dynamic balance.* Populations also exhibit certain statistical properties which are measured in terms of numbers of individuals. Such properties include population density, distribution pattern, age structure, sex ratio,
growth rate, survival rate, and mortality rate. These properties can easily
be studied in laboratory cultures, and indeed, much of our most important
information concerning natural populations arises by inference from analysis of numerical behavior of laboratory cultures. Since the organisms are
confined and the environment is greatly simplified, however, laborato-
ry-derived population data must be interpreted with some caution.

Population growth—If one introduces a number of fruit flies into a laboratory culture jar, the number of flies in the jar can change only by the
addition of individuals through *birth* or by the subtraction of individuals
through *death.* If the births and deaths are equal, the population level remains stable. If one or the other factor predominates, the population level
will respond accordingly. Here again we encounter the dynamic balance.

Numerically speaking, the size of the population at the end of time
t is the original population modified by the birth-death factor. This fact
is expressed simply in the following equation:

$$N_t = N_0 + (b\text{--}d)$$

Births and deaths may be expressed in a time-relative sense, i.e., as
birth and *death rates.* This means the number born or dying within a unit
of time. Births and deaths may also be expressed in relation to the individuals present in the population, e.g., number of births or deaths per one,
ten, or thousand individuals in the population.

Let us now define the factor r as the *instantaneous rate of change of the
population per individual already present in the population.* Obviously, r will represent the difference between the instantaneous birth and death rates, each
expressed in reference to the average individual in the population, and
the value of r may be either positive or negative. Positive values will result
in population increase, negative values lead to population decrease. The
first equation may now be restated in a more meaningful and informative
way as follows:

$$N_t = N_0 \cdot e^{rt}$$

where e is the base of the natural logarithms, and the remaining terms
are as given in the first equation. The critical feature of this equation is
the clear indication that the factor for population change, i.e., the factor
r, serves as an exponent in the equation. This is the true significance of
the factor, because *without environmental restriction population tends to change
in exponential fashion.* An increase in one generation leads to a greater increase

in the next generation, and so on. The numerical behavior of any population for several different values of r is given in Figure 3.3.

This figure is based upon the assumption that the factor r remains constant, but r can never remain constant for very many generations. A positive value would eventually lead to an infinitely large population, whereas a negative value would eventually lead to extinction. Populations

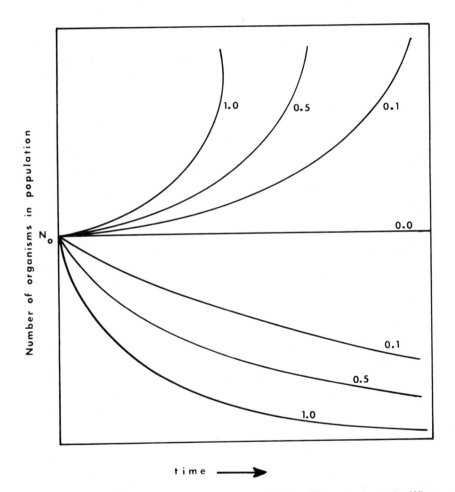

Figure 3.3. Population size in relation to time for different values of r. When r is zero, the population remains at the initial level (i.e., at N_0). When r is positive, the population increases. When r is negative, the population decreases. Logarithmic population increase (i.e., exhibiting positive values of r) can occur only in unlimited environments or in limited environments for only short periods of time.

do become extinct, but they never increase without limits. The upper boundary on population numbers is imposed by two factors, properties inherent in the organisms themselves and properties of the environment in which the population dwells.

Let us continue to assume that we are dealing with laboratory organisms and that they are being reared in containers of finite dimensions. As the population level increases, the *population density* (number of organisms per unit area) also increases. The increase in density, in turn, raises the frequency of contact between individuals. In most, if not all, species of organisms some moderate density is more favorable to the group than a very low density. Location of sex partners, opportunity for social interaction, and enhancement of group survival values all increase as the population gains from low to moderate levels. Many species do better in flocks, herds, schools, clumps, and groves than they do alone.

Nevertheless, for every species for which the matter has been investigated, problems begin to arise as the population increases above the optimum level. In the fruit flies, for example, contact between individuals becomes so frequent that the females become disturbed and cease laying eggs. In flour beetles, the adults are cannibalistic, preying upon their own eggs and young. When population levels are low, the contacts are rare, and many of the young survive. In dense populations, however, contacts are frequent, and predation becomes so intense that few young reach the pupal stage. The flour beetles also produce certain waste products which accumulate in the flour and further restrict the populations at high densities.

Density-induced stress has been investigated in some detail in confined mouse populations. As the population density increases and individual contacts become more frequent, the population tends to level off and eventually to achieve a somewhat stable size. The factor r approaches zero, not so much from adult mortality (which remains rather stable), but due to reproductive failure. At high population densities, puberty is delayed, fetal mortality rises, litter size decreases, infant survival declines (probably as a result of starvation from nonlactating mothers), and the very few young which do survive to reach the adult population just about balance the deaths due to old age and other factors.

The mechanisms by which this "self-regulation" take place have also been investigated. The stress of increased contact affects the central nervous system which stimulates the pituitary gland to release a hormone ACTH *(adrenocorticotrophin)*. This hormone stimulates growth of the adrenal cortex, particularly the *zona fasciculata* which enlarges and produces certain cortical steroid hormones. These steroids affect the body in many ways, among which is their tendency to inhibit production of certain sex hormones. Thus, primary and secondary sex characteristics are partially suppressed, puberty is delayed, and sexual activity may be restricted. These and other symptoms represent the stress disease which is displayed by many species of mammals under confinement. Evidence of this disease has also been uncovered in certain wild mammal populations under conditions of extreme crowding, and the importance of this factor in the self-regulation of many wild populations is strongly suspected, especially in cases where normal regulatory mechanisms (predators, etc.) have been eliminated.

As stated earlier populations do not increase without limit. In nature, in the absence of severe climatic fluctuations, many populations tend to maintain reasonably stable levels of balance between reproduction and mortality. This stability clearly depends, in part, upon internal factors. External biological factors such as predation, parasitism, disease, and starvation as well as the various climatic factors take their toll both by directly reducing the numbers and by imposing additional stress. As a general rule it may be said that *every species is probably capable of self-regulation at some population density, but* that *external environmental factors generally act to regulate populations at levels below those at which self-regulation would be the chief factor* (see Figure 3.4). Even at somewhat lower densities, however, self-stress factors must play a part. Population growth, instead of being a "J-shaped" curve rising to infinity, actually assumes an "S-shaped" or sigmoid form, since it tends to level off at a certain density. This stable density has often been viewed as the *carrying capacity* of the particular environment for the species in question.

Populations in nature—In the above discussion, emphasis has been placed upon population density rather than total population size because size makes sense only when the area of occupiable habitat is considered. Furthermore, the individual organism is only concerned with and influenced by those factors in its immediate surroundings. Actually, group size *per se* is of some importance in certain species of social insects, fishes, birds, and mammals where the stability of the group diminishes as the number increases beyond a certain level. In such situations, a large group may break into two or more smaller units which become independent.

In natural populations of most higher organisms, a certain maximum density level is maintained in the optimal habitat. Among plant species this density is seldom exceeded because of competition for nutrients, water, and light. In some cases the plants actually release antibiotic chemicals into the soil which prevent neighbors from becoming established too close. Among animals the density control may result from aggressive interaction which occurs during the normal search for food, shelter, and reproductive partners. In other cases, especially among the higher vertebrates, the stronger individuals actually defend territories, excluding the weaker members, thus maintaining a stable density in the more desirable habitat.

In any event among animal populations, as the optimal habitat becomes saturated, the excess individuals (especially the young) move into peripheral

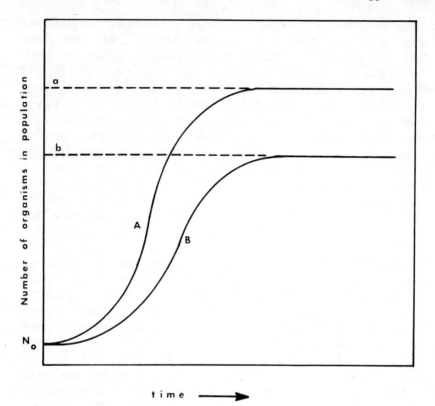

Number of organisms in population

a

b

A

B

N_o

time ⟶

Figure 3.4. Sigmoid population-growth curves characteristic of limited environments. A. Population growth achieved where the population itself is the primary regulatory factor. B. Population growth achieved where restriction is due chiefly to external environmental regulatory factors. Note the difference between the final carrying capacities *a* and *b*.

areas where they are often subject to greater environmental hazards. It has often been stated that predation and other mortality factors are proportional to overpopulation rather than to actual population size. Some mortality occurs at all population levels even in the best of environments, but for a great many species the statement is clearly true.

In laboratory cultures population size and density are determined solely by births and deaths. Field populations, however, are generally not so confined. The individuals are free to enter and leave, and these movements may influence numerical characteristics of the populations. It has already been noted that organisms move into suboptimal habitats and that they may eventually cross barriers into other populations bringing new genetic material. In many species of insects (e.g., locusts) and in some species of mammals (lemmings), high population density often leads to a dramatic mass exodus of individuals, leaving behind a population of much reduced density.

Population stability—Density levels in natural populations reflect a balance between population increase factors (birth and immigration) and population decrease factors (death and emigration). It was stated earlier that population levels also reflect a balance between internal and external factors (internal including birth, emigration, and some of the mortality and external factors including immigration and the remainder of the mortality). This is too simplistic a view, however, because as we have seen, internal and external factors often work together. Individuals weakened by intraspecific competition have lowered resistance to disease, whereas those weakened by disease make poor competitors. Individuals forced into suboptimal habitat by internal factors become exposed to increased predation, weather stress, and starvation. The stress which reduces reproduction may arise from internal or external factors, or indeed, a combination of the two. The internal-external factor balance does exist, but it operates at a very basic level and often in very subtle ways.

All things considered, just how do these factors balance out in the end? How stable are natural populations? In truth, the ecologist can point to populations with all degrees of stability from those which fluctuate wildly to those which seem to deviate little over periods of tens if not hundreds of years. Analysis of this problem in light of what has been said before leads to considerable insight into the real nature of population adjustment in relation to environmental situations.

Many species of organisms have become adapted to exploit transient environments. In this context the limits of the optimal environment are defined as much by time as by space. The organisms in question are the bacteria, microscopic aquatic organisms, protozoans, certain other lower invertebrates, insects, and to some extent, small mammals. All are characterized by small size, short life cycle, high reproductive rate, ability to move or be transported from one area to another, and possession of a physiologically inactive and environmentally inert life history stage which permits them to "sleep through" unfavorable periods. When appropriate environmental conditions prevail, they literally explode in a burst of numbers, and after a brief period of population flowering, they become physiologically dormant or die down to maintain themselves thereafter at low density levels while awaiting the next opportunity. These organisms specialize in reproduction, and once conditions become just right, their capacity for increase completely outstrips the capabilities of all outside regulatory factors. During the periods of "bloom," they often achieve fantastic population levels which are followed by the crash due to a combination of nutrient exhaustion, epidemic disease, heavy predation, and the ultimate operation of the stress syndrome. For such species distribution is seldom a problem since they are transported widely by wind and water currents or by their own locomotion, and they can remain relatively dormant in a wide variety of environments. Only a few are required to initiate a new population, and in fact, since many can reproduce asexually, a new population could conceivably be initiated by a single individual.

At the other extreme lie the stable organisms whose populations vary little year after year. These, by and large, are the larger organisms, the trees and the larger vertebrates. Space is important; time means little to an elephant or a redwood, for example. These tend toward large size, long life, slow reproductive rate, low mobility, and less physiological withdrawal. These organisms appear to have adjusted to the major climatic and soil factors. Enemies are few, and within the primary habitat areas, population regulation must be largely an internal affair. Reproduction is largely sexual, and colonization is relatively rare.

Between these two extremes lie the remainder of the species in the plant and animal kingdoms. Stability varies from one species to another and from one time to another. Even the nature of the stability exhibits variation. We may think of stability as a measure of deviation from the long-term average density. Sometimes this deviation is irregular as though fluctuating in random fashion. In other instances it is regular or sinusoidal, in the nature of an oscillation. In all cases, however, it is somewhat artificial to consider population variability, growth, density, and stability apart from the natural ecosystems of which the species are a functional part. The life history patterns and numerical characteristics have real meaning only within the overall dynamic framework of nature.

Suggestions for Further Reading

ANDREWARTHA, H. G. *Introduction to the Study of Animal Populations*. Chicago: The University of Chicago Press, 1961.

CHRISTIAN, J. J., and DAVIS, D. E. "Endocrines, behavior, and populations." *Science*, vol. 146, 1964.

ELTON, C. *Animal Ecology*. New York: MacMillan Co., 1939.

LACK, D. "Darwin's Finches." *Scientific American*, April 1953.

————. *The Natural Regulation of Animal Numbers*. London: Oxford University Press, 1954.

MALTHUS, THOMAS R. *An Essay on the Principle of Population*. London: Johnson, 1798.

MAYR, E. *Systematics and the Origin of Species*. New York: Columbia University Press, 1942.

SIMPSON, G. G., and BECK, W. S. *Life: An Introduction to Biology*. 2nd ed. New York: Harcourt, Brace and World, 1965.

VOLPE, E. P. *Understanding Evolution*. Dubuque, Iowa: Wm. C. Brown Co. Publishers, 1967.

WYNNE-EDWARDS, V. C. "Population Control in Animals." *Scientific American*, August 1964.

4. the
community

Introduction

Any given area is inhabited by populations belonging to a great many different species. Counting all the various types of microbes, tiny soil organisms, and larger plants and animals, hundreds if not thousands of species may be found in a single virgin forest or prairie. Living close together, these species interact with one another in a variety of ways, sometimes harmful, sometimes beneficial, and in some cases by absolute dependence upon one another. Most of these species have been in close contact with each other for thousands of generations; they have, in fact, undergone much of their evolutionary history together, and the myriads of subtle interrelationships result from the constant mutual genetic adjustment whereby a total system is fashioned from independent parts. This multi-species system is called the *natural community*.

A community is a functional species aggregate of any size. The rotting oak log, the prairie pond, and the oyster reef comprise small communities, whereas the oak forest, the prairie, and the sea are large communities. Regardless of size, however, every natural community includes a characteristic array of species, each functioning in its own way, and each contributing in some manner to the overall long-range stability of the total system, i.e., to the *balance of nature*.

The natural community operates within the context of a physical environment, and it has already been pointed out that the major physical factors determine, in great measure, the type of community which comes to occupy an area. Recalling that each organism modifies its own immediate surroundings, however, it follows that each community tends to shape the overall

43

environment in certain characteristic ways. The soil and, to some extent, the atmospheric conditions reflect the type of community which clothes the region, and indeed, if the community is removed, both the soil and the local climate are affected.

It is somewhat unrealistic to consider plant without soil or soil without plant or plant-soil without atmosphere. To understand the complex community-environment relationships, however, it is first necessary to examine the community itself in some detail.

Community Structure

Upon entering a wet tropical forest (as we did in the prologue), one is at first bewildered by the size, grandeur, diversity, and complexity of the living panorama. Man is a dwarf in this forest; it literally "swallows" him. It towers over his head, it twists and tangles all around, and visibility is everywhere limited to a few feet. But even in such a forest where nature reaches her zenith, through painstaking (and sometimes painful) work, man is able to discern certain basic structural and functional patterns by which the remarkable system operates.

Community structure may be visualized in two ways. The first is more anatomical and geographic. It concerns forms, sizes, and patterns of distribution of the system components. The second view relates more to the functional organization — the assembly lines by which materials and energy are passed through the system and the pathways of communication which bind the system into a functional whole. These views will be referred to respectively as the anatomical and the organizational structure of the community.

Community anatomy — Focusing first upon the anatomy, one notes that the community is composed of structural units, the individual species. Each displays a characteristic size and *life form* (tree, vine, shrub, ground plant, fish, mammal, bird, etc.) which may often be recognized by the untrained observer. These sizes and life forms together form a community with vertical depth, and within this context there is a definite layering or vertical stratification. In both terrestrial and aquatic communities, the layering effect is due chiefly to the vertical patterns of the major plants as they have become adjusted to the light factor of the environment. In the forest there may be many layers: the crown of the forest giants, general tree canopy, two or more layers of smaller trees, bushes, ground surface, and subsoil (Figure 4.1). Within the general framework established by the major vegetation, the smaller plant and animal species find their own stratified *microhabitats* — the monkeys, birds, and mosquitoes of the forest crown; the bromeliads, orchids, and vine snakes of lower tree branches; the tree frogs, beetles, and snails of the small trees; the deer, peccaries, rodents, toads, and other

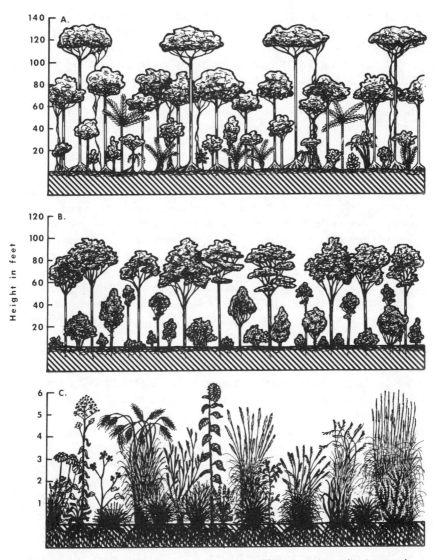

Figure 4.1. Vertical stratification in three different community types. A. Tropical rain forest. This highly developed system exhibits a complex and well-defined pattern of vertical layering. B. Temperate zone forest. Although less complex than the rain forest and lacking the overstory of very tall trees, this system also exhibits recognizable layers. C. Tall prairie, including grasses and a variety of types of herbaceous plants. Careful inspection reveals rather well-defined strata even in the prairie system. Within a given system, the different layers provide slightly different microenvironments which are ecologically important to the species utilizing them.

ground dwellers; the snakes, insects, worms, and microbes of the subsoil — each to its own layer. Some species, such as the leaf-cutting ants, however, make regular or periodic use of more than one layer.

Another feature of the anatomy of the community is the horizontal patterns by which the organisms of a given species distribute themselves throughout the landscape. Some are scattered about as though at random; others tend to space themselves out in rather regular fashion (like trees in an orchard); but most live in some sort of clumps or aggregates, and these aggregates may themselves show certain recognizable patterns of distribution. For any given species there tends to be a characteristic average density, both within the group and across the landscape. In tropical forests the trees are very dense, but this profusion stems from a great variety of species, and each species is relatively rare within any given sampling area. The reverse is true in forests of the cold temperate regions where the major vegetation consists of dense populations of a few species.

From one type of community to another, the species composition differs. Consequently, the manifestations of size, shape, density, and horizontal and vertical pattern differ. Each community type displays a somewhat unique structural personality, but regardless of whether one is considering a forest or a prairie, a pond or an ocean, the basic anatomy represents but variations on the above themes.

Nutritional organization of the community — In the lives of all organisms, the matter of nutrition is foremost, and for the great majority of species, it is a matter of rather constant concern. In treating the functional organization of natural communities, therefore, the nutritional organization must be considered paramount. Green plants alone are capable of converting radiant energy of the sun into high-energy chemical bonds of organic compounds. They alone can convert carbon dioxide and minerals into living protoplasm. These are the *producers* of the organic material. All the other members of the community (microbes, nongreen plants, and animals) are nutritionally dependent upon the green plants and are called *consumers*.

As illustrated in Table 4.1, the consumers may be subdivided into several overlapping groups depending upon their primary nutrient source. They may also be arranged in a series based upon the number of nutritional steps they are removed from the basic food source, the green plants. Herbivores, which feed directly on the plants, are called *primary consumers*. Animals which eat the herbivores are called *secondary consumers*, and so on. Thus, within every natural community, one may discern *food chains* (leaf-earthworm-worm snake-coral snake; grass-grasshopper-field mouse-hawk; algae-copepod-fish larva-menhaden-mackerel). Within every community there are many food chains, and since the consumers are often not very finicky about their diets, these food chains interlock to form complex *food webs* (Figure 4.2). It has been found that change in the abundance of one

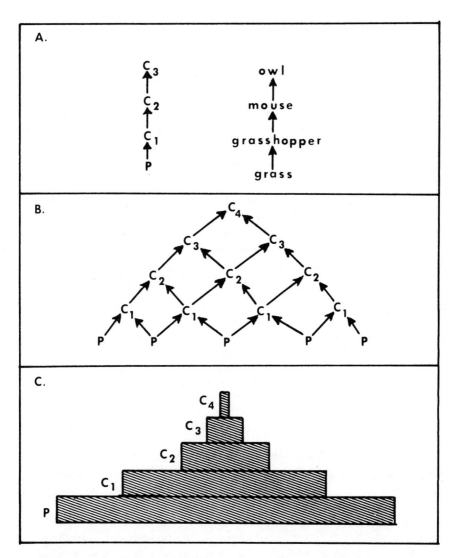

Figure 4.2. Three ways of interpreting the nutritional organization of natural communities. A. The simple food chain containing a single element at each of the four levels. Some high-Arctic food chains are nearly this simple. B. The food web. In most food webs the number of elements at a given level progressively diminishes as one proceeds toward the apex. C. The food pyramid. In this type of diagram, emphasis is placed upon the relative amount of material (or energy) tied up in each level, irrespective of the number of elements present at the level. In all the figures, *P* indicates producers and *C* consumers.

TABLE 4.1

Classification	Explanation
I. Producers	Plants which do not depend upon preexisting organic material. They subsist and produce protoplasm from carbon dioxide, water, minerals, and non-organic energy sources.
A. Autotrophs	Plants which utilize sunlight as an energy source by means of a photo-pigment such as *chlorophyll.* Autotrophs include all green plants and many lower plants, such as algae and bacteria, which may be blue-green, red, brown, golden, or yellow in color (depending upon the particular photo-pigments they contain).
B. Chemotrophs	Plants which derive their energy through the oxidation of non-organic chemical compounds. These are mostly bacteria which lack photo-pigments, and the chief compounds which they attack are ammonia, nitrites, sulfides, elemental sulfur, and ferrous iron salts.
II. Consumers	Animals, colorless lower plants, and certain microorganisms which depend entirely upon previously formed organic material for their energy source. The consumer species do not always fit into the neat classification system. Many feed upon several types of organic material, and some shift from one food type to another depending upon food availability.
A. Herbivores	Animals which feed primarily upon living plants. These are sometimes called *primary consumers* since they are only one step removed from the producers.

TABLE 4.1 continued

B. Carnivores   Animals which depend largely upon other living
                    animals for their food. These may also be called
                    secondary, tertiary, etc. *consumers,* depending upon
                    how many nutritional steps they are removed from
                    the producers. Carnivores are often divided into two
                    categories, but the distinctions are not always obvious.

  1. Predators   Animals which tend to kill and eat their prey. They
                    are often larger than the prey, have simple life his-
                    tories, are relatively unspecialized, and are not par-
                    ticular about what species of prey animal they at-
                    tack.

  2. Parasites   Animals which tend to be much smaller than their
                    hosts, to live upon or within their hosts, and to feed
                    slowly upon host tissues over a longer period of time.
                    Parasite life histories are often quite complex, involv-
                    ing a different host for each of several life history
                    stages. Anatomy and physiology may be highly
                    specialized for the parasitic way of life. Many para-
                    sites have very specific host requirements.

C. Multivores   Animals which feed upon a variety of plant and
                    animal materials and which do not fall naturally
                    into the herbivore or carnivore categories. Man is
                    a multivore.

D. Decomposers   Mostly microscopic organisms (bacteria, fungi,
                    and some of the smaller invertebrates) which sub-
                    sist largely or entirely upon dead organic matter.
                    These decay organisms "mineralize" the organic
                    material, releasing end products which may be
                    reused by the producer species.

species in a food web may be reflected by adjustments up and down a given chain and across the web in other chains. One example will serve to illustrate the case. In years when the Wisconsin quail population is especially dense and spilling over into suboptimal habitat, the eggs, young, and adults provide a feast for all manner of consumers, many of which would never catch a quail in an ordinary year. During years when quail are especially scarce, the owls and other forms which normally prey upon quail are forced to search elsewhere creating pressures on other portions of the food web.

Although food chains interlock into remarkably complex webs, in terrestrial communities, at least, no food chain is known to be more than four or five steps in length from producer to top consumer. There seem to be two explanations. In the first place, the consumer is never completely efficient in harvesting the food crop. Fortunately, some remains around to form the crop for the next year. Some may be inedible, and so on. In the second place, the consumer is never able to convert all the ingested food into its own protoplasm. Some is indigestible and is eliminated as fecal material; much is eliminated as urinary or other discarded material; and a great deal is burned as fuel in the process of respiration. The combination of low harvest efficiency and low metabolic efficiency means that in natural populations the consumer species is able, at best, to convert only 5 to 20 percent of the food resource into its own protoplasm. Often the percentage is far less. Although food webs may be very broad, especially at the lower levels, because of the accumulated inefficiencies, they can never be very long. Top predators such as sharks, mountain lions, and eagles are so scarce that it would not pay to have another predator level above them.

In addition to the more spectacular predator chains, there are parasite and decomposer chains. Many parasitic forms are known to support *hyperparasites*. The rat flea *Xenopsylla cheopis* is host to the bacterium *Bacillus pestis* (which causes bubonic plague when it accidentally gets into humans). The turkey may carry a nematode worm which harbors a disease-producing microbe. Parasitism and hyperparasitism are widespread in nature, but again such chains are relatively short.

Decomposer chains are poorly understood. Most decomposer organisms are relatively small, hard to identify, and even more difficult to work with. Their diversity is astounding. Hence, despite their obvious importance, ecologists have generally neglected this difficult and specialized field. We do, however, know a few things about decomposers. Decomposition of an organic structure, such as a piece of wood, involves both mechanical and chemical processes. Larger organisms (rodents, insects, worms, etc.) are valuable in the mechanical reduction of the material to smaller pieces, and through their tunneling activities they distribute microbes and permit air and moisture to penetrate throughout the wood. The microbes are biochemical specialists. They secrete enzymes into the environment (i.e., into the wood) which break down the large chemical molecules and eventually demineralize and oxidize the smaller fragments. Complete decomposition of a piece of wood involves the action of many specialized microbes working in tandem teams, each member carrying out its own specific chemical task.

The number of nutritional steps involved and the microbial efficiencies are not known, but it is clear that decomposer chains often interlock with other consumer chains. The robin eats the earthworm; the bear demolishes the decaying log for beetle grubs. Moreover, in shallow-water aquatic communities, the decomposers support thriving bottom fish and invertebrate chains which become linked at the higher consumer levels with the algae-based food chains of the upper water strata. In habitats devoid of light (caves and the deep sea), producers are absent, and the fish and invertebrate communities are presumed to be totally supported by decomposer chains deriving their nourishment from imported organic matter.

We have seen that the nutritional structure of the community is based upon the types and numbers of food chains making up the food web. Such webs often show many species near the base and fewer in the higher levels. Considering that the lower levels generally represent the more abundant species (in terms of numbers and weight), it is clear that the food web really represents some sort of *food pyramid* (Figure 4.2). Thus, at any one moment the greatest amount of material (*standing crop*) is present in the producer organisms. Primary consumers contain less, secondary consumers even less, and so on. The reduction is essentially logarithmic so that the top consumer contains an infinitely small standing crop in comparison with the amount present in the producers. This pyramid model emphasizes the reduction in amount at each consumer step, but it ignores the parasite and decomposer chains, and in research practice it is next to impossible to fit many species into neat consumer levels.

Communication and community structure — In a sense, the nutrition network represents a communication system which ramifies through the community. Nutritional exchange transmits messages of organizational information from one species population to another. For example, information concerning the abundance of quail is transmitted to the local rodent populations in terms of heavy or light predation by hungry or well-fed owls. The careful observer realizes that other types of information are also transferred among the organisms of nature. Much of this information is carried by chemicals (*pheromones*) whose importance is the message *per se*, and not nutrition. The odors of nature have meaning. Ants leave chemical trails for other ants to follow. Many mammals (especially rodents and members of the dog, cat, and weasel families) mark their territories with urine. Females of many species release specific sex attractants which permit males of the same species to locate sex partners in a world of diversity. Such chemical messages have particular meaning for other members of the same species, and they aid in the integration of group activity and the maintenance of group integrity.

Communication may also be accomplished by sound, light, coloration, special marking, and behavior patterns. Despite poetic considerations, birds do not always sing from pure joy. Territorial defense, mate attraction, recognition, alarm, and other messages are conveyed. Neither do lions roar, jaguars growl, porpoises squeak, frogs croak, and crickets trill for purely esthetic reasons. Hydrophones reveal that the oceans are very noisy places, and the U.S. Navy has spent large sums of money trying to decipher this crackling, grunting, squealing symphony of the sea. Careful analysis suggests that many, if not most, animal sounds serve strictly utilitarian intraspecific functions of attraction, repulsion, species recognition, intimidation, warning, fear, and echo-location. The same may be said for the light-flashing of the firefly.

When two members of the same species meet, interesting behavior patterns are often displayed. These patterns may signal recognition, bluff, challenge, or dominance-subordination, or they may represent the prelude to mating or combat. Although obviously important in communication within the species, such signals may also provide information to other species. The jaguar follows the scent of the deer, the deer is panicked by the growl of the jaguar, the snake is attracted by the toad chorus, the predatory boring snail "homes-in" on the chemicals released by the oyster. The bright color, fragrance, and even the shape of the flower is often simply adaptation for the attraction and accommodation of the pollinating insect or hummingbird.

Just as the community is bound together by an integrated food web, so it is meshed by a web of subtle signals and cues. Science is still only dimly aware of the "conversations" of nature, but we know enough to realize that they are constantly in progress, that they are meaningful both within and between species, and that some measure of population and community regulation may be expected from this source.

Community Function

In the above discussion it has been necessary to consider some function in relation to organization. There remains the problem of quantitative community metabolism. Involved in this matter are rates of production, storage, and utilization of carbon, minerals, and energy. These topics can be most effectively treated within the framework of the ecosystem. Hence, their consideration will be reserved for the next chapter.

Community Development

Less than a hundred thousand years ago most of North America above the Ohio and Missouri Rivers was blanketed with a deep layer of glacial ice, and much of Canada and the north-central states as far south as Chicago was covered as recently as eight or nine thousand years ago. Yet when Europeans first set foot on North American soil, they were met, not by ice, but by dense forests. In the west were high and low prairies, and in the far north the low treeless tundra (Figure 4.3). The lakes and streams were teeming with plant, invertebrate, and fish life. How did it happen? How did the living communities invade the bare rock, the bleak piles of glacial rubble, and the sterile ponds left stark and naked by the retreating ice? The unfolding of this remarkable story is one of the more interesting detective tales of recent scientific investigation.

Upon its retreat the glacier exposed a variety of bare area types: cliffs and valleys; rolling landscape of rocks, boulders, sand, and powdery "rock flour"; lakes, streams, and ponds. The invaders came by many means. Most of the smaller forms (possessing physiologically inactive stages) were probably sown by the wind, as were the seeds of the larger plants. The larger land animals must have come under their own power carrying with them, no doubt, seeds, parasites, and an assortment of small social creatures in their feathers and fur. By whatever means, many mobile species quickly moved into the new habitat; others are still moving north.

Doubtless, most of the new immigrants were unsuccessful. Only those hardy pioneering forms which could withstand the extreme conditions of the bare areas flourished and reproduced at first. Generation after generation their remains accumulated and decomposed, adding organic matter to the mineral substratum. A thin soil was formed. Other species could now survive, and as these came in, the old pioneers were crowded out. With continued enrichment of the soil and more shading of the ground, additional new species could survive, each group, in turn, replacing the old, from a few small scattered pioneers to creeping ground shrubs and grasses to bushes, low trees, to tall forest. With each group of species came soil enrichment and further amelioration of near-ground atmospheric conditions. Finally there arrived a group of species in which the young could survive with the elders. Community change became imperceptibly slow. The mature community had been achieved; the forest, the mature prairie, the tundra.

Each species is adapted to survive within a given range of environmental conditions. The pioneers alone could withstand the extremes of heat, light, and moisture and the shifting substratum devoid of organic matter. But the pioneers could not tolerate competition from the invaders which entered the modified environment. Each group of species created

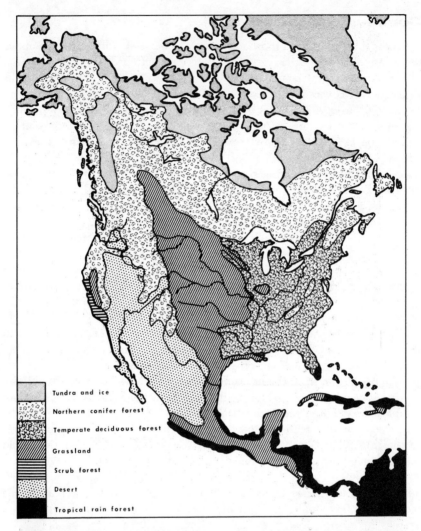

Figure 4.3. Native vegetational communities of North America. Note the close relationship between the distribution of vegetation, climate (Figure 2.3.), and soil types (Figure 2.5.). As a rule, climate is considered to be the primary factor controlling vegetational distribution, although on a local level sometimes the nature of the substratum may play a major role. (Adapted from *Climate and Man*, 1941 Yearbook of Agriculture.)

conditions more favorable for their successors, and each, in turn, was eliminated as the soil became richer and more stabilized and as the above-ground
environment became more shady, more humid, and less variable. This
process of regular species replacement and environmental modification is
known as *community succession* (Figure 4.4).

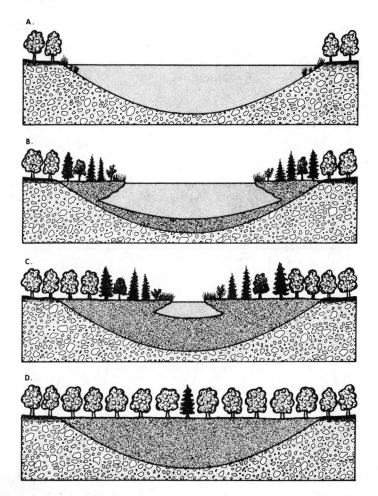

Figure 4.4. An example of community succession—the *hydrosere* (i.e., community development from a lake to a mature regional-climax forest). A. Young lake stage. The lake, which has recently been formed by some geological event, has been invaded by fishes and other aquatic organisms, and the margins support both submerged and emergent aquatic vegetation. B. Developing bog stage. The lake bottom is being filled with organic materials which rain down from the waters above. Marginal encroachment is proceeding by the build-out of the boggy edge. Note the regular progression of plant species (sedges, bog willows, spruce, bog birch, and tamarack are figured). C. Late bog stage. Bottom filling and marginal encroachment have nearly eliminated the open water. Upland forest has already become established on what was formerly part of the lake. D. Late subclimax forest stage. Regional-climax forest has almost completely replaced the earlier bog forest. The developmental scheme depicted is broadly representative of lake-bog succession in the glaciated areas of the northern United States and Canada from Maine and the Maritime Provinces on the east to Minnesota and the Prairie Provinces on the west.

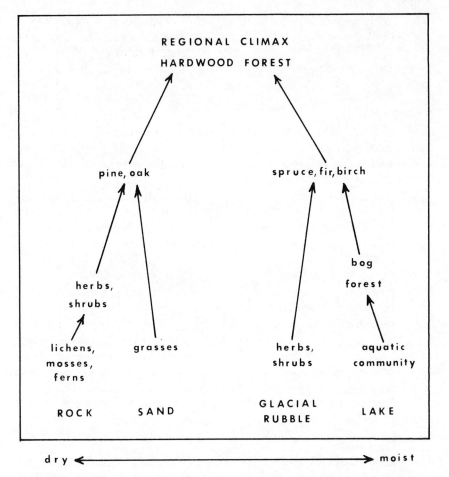

REGIONAL CLIMAX

HARDWOOD FOREST

pine, oak · spruce, fir, birch

herbs, shrubs

bog forest

lichens, mosses, ferns · grasses · herbs, shrubs · aquatic community

ROCK · SAND · GLACIAL RUBBLE · LAKE

dry ← → moist

Figure 4.5. The pattern of regional community succession in the northern states and southern Canada. Regardless of the initial type of bare area (rock, sand, glacial rubble, or water), development proceeds toward the same regional climax community. Note that the early stages are strongly influenced by the type of substratum, but that as the soil builds up, the vegetation becomes more closely controlled by the regional climatic conditions. All subcommunity developmental sequences tend toward the regional-climax type, which in the present case is hardwood forest.

Within the formerly glaciated area of the United States and Canada and especially around the Great Lakes, the phenomenon of community succession has been studied in exhaustive detail. Pollen and other remains taken from peat bogs and lake bottoms and dated by the radiocarbon method provide an actual record of the major events. Succession still in progress furnishes the detail.

For any type of bare area, the sequence of species and stages is quite regular and is now predictable. During early stages of succession, the community tends to reflect the nature of the parent substrate, but within a given region, as succession proceeds, all the developmental types tend to develop toward the same mature community which is, therefore, known as the regional climax community (Figure 4.5). In southeastern Wisconsin it is the maple-beech-basswood, in northern Wisconsin the maple-beech-hemlock, around Lake Superior the spruce fir, in southwestern Wisconsin and western Minnesota it is the tall prairie. The climate determines the nature of the climax community, and the climate and the community together determine the soil characteristics.

These general conclusions apply to community succession throughout the world, but there are exceptions. Some soils are so charged with minerals that the climatic climax cannot be achieved. Around hills and canyons the slope and exposure or protection from sunlight may be the overriding considerations. Ponds, marshes, and shallow lakes tend to become filled with organic remains, and they develop thereafter as terrestrial communities. But certain infertile deep lakes have accumulated only an inch or so of sediment since the last glacier's retreat.

The factors of succession are also the processes involved in wound healing. If the tree canopy is broken by windfalls, early successional stages quickly move in to repair the damage. Devastation resulting from severe forest or prairie fire is followed by successional redevelopment. In most natural communities, the species characteristic of the various successional stages are generally present somewhere, and the damage is repaired quickly from within.

Suggestions for Further Reading

BARNETT, L., and the editorial staff of *Life. The World We Live In.* New York: Time Inc., 1955.

BROWN, W. L.; EISNER, L. T.; and WHITTAKER, R. H.; "Allomones and Kairomones: Transspecific Chemical Messengers." *BioScience,* vol. 20, 1970.

DARWIN, CHARLES, R. *The Origin of Species by Means of Natural Selection or the Preservation of Favored Races in the Struggle for Life.* London: Murray, 1859.

DICE, L. R. *The Biotic Provinces of North America.* Ann Arbor: University of Michigan Press, 1952.

HAMBRIDGE, G. *Climate and Man.* Washington, D.C.: U.S. Department of Agriculture (Yearbook), 1941.

HAZEN, W. E. *Readings in Population and Community Ecology.* Philadelphia: W. B. Saunders Co., 1970.

KENDEIGH, S. C. *Animal Ecology.* Englewood Cliffs, N. J.: Prentice-Hall, Inc., 1961.

ODUM, E. P. *Fundamentals of Ecology.* Philadelphia: W. B. Saunders Co., 1971.

PEARSE, A. S. *Animal Ecology.* New York: McGraw-Hill Book Co., 1939.

SHELFORD, V. E. *Animal Communities in Temperate America.* Chicago: University of Chicago Press, 1913.

5. the

ecosystem

The water, carbon, nitrogen, phosphorus, sulfur, iron, and other chemical materials which today are bound up in living protoplasm will tomorrow be part of the environment. "All go unto one place; all are of the dust, and all turn to dust again" (Eccl. III, 20). For over two thousand years man has comprehended the cycles of nature in a general way. Yet, incomplete as our knowledge still is, our present appreciation is new and different.

With the aid of radioactive isotopes, we are beginning to understand the chemical cycles in marvelous detail, to keep track of the residence times of each type of chemical in the various "pools" and "reservoirs" of nature, and to measure the rates of turnover, i.e., the speed with which the materials move from one pool to another. Most important, the chemical cycles are now being considered in relation to the basic principles which govern energy transformation in the universe. The organism-environment complex which embraces the complete chemical cycle is known as the *ecosystem. So intimately are the community and environment bound together in the physical, chemical, and biological cycles of the natural world that the ecosystem is considered the basic functional unit of nature,* and the ecosystem concept is, without a doubt, the most unique, far-reaching, and important contribution the field of ecology has made to human knowledge.

Biogeochemical Cycles

The term *biogeochemical* reflects the fact that the circulating chemicals are associated with both living and nonliving portions of the ecosystem. Of the ninety-or-so chemical elements which occur naturally in the air, soil, rocks, and waters of the earth only thirty or forty are known to be required by living organisms, and over half of these are needed in only trace amounts. The *biogenic* elements thus fall into major and minor categories based upon the quantities required by organisms comprising the natural communities.

All chemical elements differ in their physical properties, in their behavior toward other types of chemicals, and in their roles in relation to the living systems. The different chemical elements display distinct personalities, and, therefore, the biogeochemical cycle of every element is in many respects unique. For each element there exist one or more major environmental "reservoirs" where the element is stored in quantity far in excess of the amount normally bound up in living systems, and often the "reservoir" can only be tapped slowly and with great difficulty. For most elements the biologically important part is that in the *circulating state*, i.e., in readily utilizable chemical form or in easily-tapped "pools."

Despite the chemical diversity, the cycles fall naturally into two categories depending upon whether one of the major reservoirs is the atmosphere (*gaseous cycle*) or whether all the reservoirs are associated with the rocks, soil, and water (*sedimentary cycle*). Both types of cycles will be considered below.

Sedimentary cycles — The phosphorus and sulfur cycles will illustrate how sedimentary cycles work, in general, and some of the differences encountered among cycles which do not involve significant atmospheric reservoirs. All biogeochemical cycles are extremely complex in detail, but their essential features may be illustrated in rather simple flow diagrams (Figure 5.1).

In both the phosphorus and sulfur cycles, the element enters the community by root absorption of the soluble oxidized anionic form (phosphate and sulfate). Within the plant both elements are incorporated into proteins, although phosphorus is employed in many other important physiological connections (ATP, DNA, RNA, phospho-lipids). Both elements pass to herbivores and carnivores through the consumer food chains. Organic compounds containing phosphorus and sulfur enter the soil through leaf-fall, secretions, metabolic wastes, and eventually, death of the organisms. Through a series of steps, the microbial decomposer chains convert the organically bound elements into soluble inorganic forms useful for higher plants. For both cycles the major terrestrial reservoir is the inorganic salts present in upland rocks. The elemental form of sulfur is of little consequence in most terrestrial ecosystems.

These two cycles appear quite similar on paper, but there are major differences. The quantity of phosphorus required by the community greatly exceeds the amount of sulfur needed, yet phosphate, which is relatively insoluble, tends to remain in the uppermost layers of the soil where it

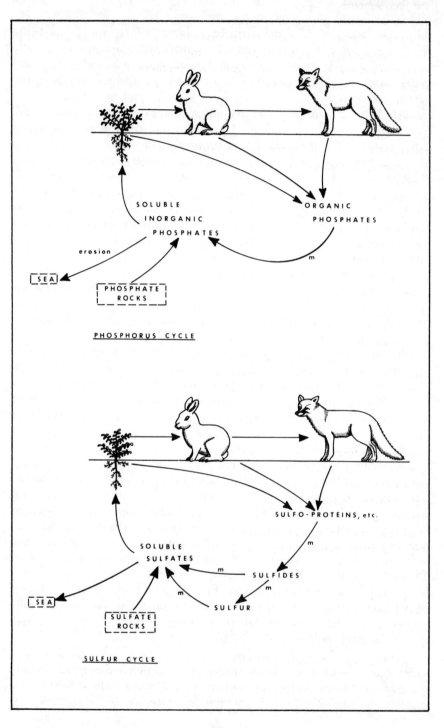

SOLUBLE
INORGANIC
PHOSPHATES

ORGANIC
PHOSPHATES

erosion

SEA

PHOSPHATE
ROCKS

m

PHOSPHORUS CYCLE

SULFO-PROTEINS, etc.

SOLUBLE
SULFATES

m

SULFIDES

m

m

SEA

m

SULFUR

SULFATE
ROCKS

m

SULFUR CYCLE

is rapidly removed by the forces of erosion. For these reasons many of the native soils are low in phosphorus, and scarcity of this important element often limits the degree of organic development in natural ecosystems. Once in the reservoir of the sea, both elements are essentially trapped, and thereafter they do not naturally reenter the terrestrial cycles except in the longterm geological sense (millions of years) as mountain ranges are lifted from the sea bottom. Some compounds of sulfur (hydrogen sulfide, sulfur dioxide, sulfur trioxide) do occur naturally in minor amounts in the atmosphere, but such amounts are negligible in terms of the overall cycles.

   Gaseous cycles — The gaseous cycles are illustrated by the nitrogen and carbon cycles (Figure 5.2). Here the situation becomes more complex. Both elements may enter the plant in the soluble ionic form (nitrate, bicarbonate), and in the case of nitrogen, this is the major pathway of entrance into the community. Once in the organism, nitrogen is used chiefly in the formation of amino acids and proteins, but it is also widely used elsewhere in lipids, photo- and respiratory pigments, structural elements, etc. Carbon abounds in all the organic compounds of the body, and together with hydrogen and oxygen, it is one of the three elements needed in highest quantity (followed closely, however, by nitrogen).

   Nitrogen and carbon both pass through the consumer chains and eventually into the soil where microbial decomposition reconverts them to the respective inorganic forms. Atmospheric nitrogen would be unavailable for plant life were it not for certain nitrogen-fixing bacteria and blue-green algae which are able to overcome a considerable energy barrier to convert elemental nitrogen to nitrate. Especially important in this connection are the nodule-forming bacteria associated with the roots of clover, alfalfa, peas, soybeans, and other leguminous plants. Nitrogen fixation is a two-way street, however, since other soil microbes convert nitrate back into elemental nitrogen. Through erosion some of the nitrate leaves the terrestrial ecosystems and is carried by the rivers into the sea, but this may be more than balanced by the nitrogen which becomes available (especially in the form of ammonia) from igneous rocks and through volcanic activity.

◀ **Figure 5.1.** Essential features of the natural biogeochemical cycles of two important chemical elements (phosphorus and sulfur) which have primarily sedimentary cycles, i.e., the atmosphere is not involved in any major way. The chief reservoirs are outlined by dashed lines. The letter *m* refers to the important roles played by decomposer microbes. As pointed out in Chapter 8, man is playing an increasing role as a major biogeochemical agent, and the sulfur cycle, in particular, has recently developed a strong atmospheric component primarily as a result of fuel combustion. (Adapted from ZoBell, 1963, and other sources.)

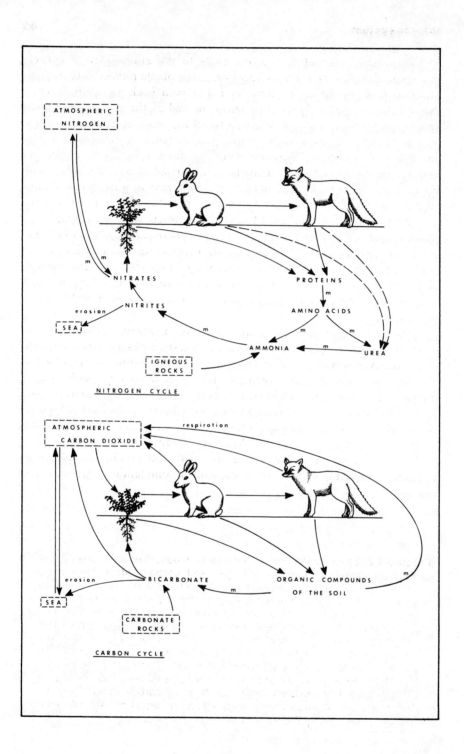

ATMOSPHERIC
NITROGEN

NITRATES

m   m

NITRITES

erosion

SEA

PROTEINS

m

AMINO ACIDS

m   m

AMMONIA   m   UREA

IGNEOUS
ROCKS

NITROGEN CYCLE

ATMOSPHERIC
CARBON DIOXIDE   respiration

erosion

SEA

BICARBONATE   m   ORGANIC COMPOUNDS
OF THE SOIL   m

CARBONATE
ROCKS

CARBON CYCLE

The relationship of the carbon cycle to the atmosphere is entirely unique. In the process of photosynthesis, green plants remove carbon dioxide directly from the atmosphere, and it is paid back gradually through the respiration of the plants themselves as well as the consumer animals and decomposer microbes. Compared to all the other cycles, carbon turnover is quite rapid, some of it returning in a matter of minutes or hours, and a large percentage of it within weeks or months. In aquatic communities, especially, the quantity actually accumulated is small in relation to the amount which turns over within a given period of time. Some soluble bicarbonate is lost temporarily to the sea, but this loss is quickly made up by the sea-air carbon dioxide exchange which aids in maintaining a constant level of carbon dioxide in the atmosphere. Carbonate rocks (limestones, dolomites, shales) abound in the earth's crust, and carbon is not likely to run short in any natural community. In contrast with the nitrogen cycle, the carbon reservoir of the atmosphere is readily tapped by the community, and atmospheric carbon dioxide forms a regular part of the carbon cycle in nature.

The above discussion has centered on the pathways by which several elements cycle through the ecosystem. In all cases rocks and the sea constitute primary reservoirs, and in some cases the atmosphere is involved in a major way. Soil and the organisms represent temporary pools, and in the case of carbon, the atmosphere is both reservoir and temporary pool. The critical role of the microorganisms must be reemphasized. These diverse and little-known forms represent both the waste disposal and nutrient regeneration systems of nature. Without a healthy soil biota, the cycles of nature would rapidly grind to a halt with the producers and higher consumers expiring in their own stagnant accumulation of garbage and sewage.

◀ **Figure 5.2.** Essential features of the natural biogeochemical cycles of two important chemical elements (nitrogen and carbon) which have major atmospheric as well as sedimentary components. Dashed lines outline the primary reservoirs, and the letter *m* indicates the steps where microbial decomposers are most important. Although nitrogen gas makes up over 78 percent of the atmosphere, this is unavailable to most plants until converted to nitrates by soil microbes. On the other hand, atmospheric carbon dioxide is directly usable by green plants. It is a matter of pure luck that man has not so far poisoned the important nitrogen-fixing bacteria through his widespread use of potent chemical pesticides. The combustion of fossil fuels has released large quantities of carbon dioxide into the atmosphere with unknown long-range effects on world climate. (Adapted from Chapman, 1931; ZoBell, 1963a; and other sources.)

Ecological Energetics

Energy and life — Energy is defined as the ability to do work (i.e., it is the force necessary to move an object a given distance, to lift a weight against the pull of gravity, to push electrons through a wire, to activate photons, to power a chemical reaction). Without the input of energy, nothing happens in either the inanimate or the animate worlds. The interior of a moon rock remains unchanged through the billions of years since the event by which it was first formed. Without a steady inflow of energy, biogeochemical cycles are "frozen."

Energy exists in many forms, and all states are interconvertible from one to another. Radiant, chemical, mechanical, and heat energy are the forms of greatest importance in relation to living systems. During every energy transformation there is an overall tendency toward degradation from a higher to a lower state. Heat, which results from the random, disorganized movement of molecules, is the lowest energy state, and all transformations are accompanied by some heat loss (i.e., friction). Thus, in passing from one state to another, no energy transformation is 100 percent efficient except those transfers in which the final state is heat. Even though the overall tendency is toward degradation, in any given transformation a fraction of the energy may be pumped to a higher state of organization, and it is this fact which permits the existence of life.

Energy in the ecosystem — Through the complicated process of photosynthesis, green plants derive energy from sunlight. A portion of this "trapped" energy goes directly into the fixation of carbon (from atmospheric carbon dioxide to organic compounds). Since the amount of energy accumulated by this process can be determined, measurement of carbon dioxide uptake provides solid information concerning this portion of the trapped solar energy. Plants also capture solar energy by at least one other pathway (ATP) which cannot be measured by the carbon uptake method. Therefore, in the present discussion (and indeed, in all current ecological work on the matter), energy values listed for the photosynthetic process must be considered minimal values.

Only a portion of the radiant energy received from the sun ever strikes a plant leaf, and of the energy which does so, only about half lies within the band of wavelengths which can activate the chlorophyll molecule. The plant, however, is not very efficient in utilizing the energy absorbed by the leaf so that, in final analysis, photosynthesis ties up only about 1 percent of the incident radiation. A portion of the captured energy goes into the fueling of the plant's metabolic processes and is subsequently lost through respiration. The remainder is retained by the plant and is accumulated as growth. This may be restated as follows:

Energy intake = energy loss (respiration) + energy retained (growth)

or:

gross production = respiration + net production

In dealing with *primary production* (i.e., plant production), one may talk in terms of energy (calories), carbon, or total biomass, but it must be made clear whether one is referring to gross or net production. The latter figure, of course, is the one which represents the food supply available for harvest by the primary consumer species.

Net primary production estimates for the major world ecosystems are presented in Table 5.1. Net production rates vary from 7 to 250 tons of carbon produced per square kilometer per year depending upon the type of ecosystem involved. For a given latitude (hence, for a given amount

TABLE 5.1

Type of ecosystem	Percent of world's surface area	Rate of production (tons C/km^2/yr)	Percent of total annual production
Forest	8.6	250	33.2
Cultivated land	5.3	149	12.9
Grassland	6.1	43	3.3
Desert	9.2	7	0.6
Total land	29.2	111	50.0
Total Ocean	70.8	46	50.0

Estimated annual net production of organic matter by the major ecosystems of the world. The total surface of the earth (ca. 510×10^6 km^2) produces an estimated 33.2×10^9 tons of organic carbon per year. Note that the average rate of production of the world's oceans (46 tons C/km^2/yr) is about the same as for the grasslands (43 tons C/km^2/yr), but this is somewhat misleading. Most of the marine production occurs on the shallow continental shelves and in certain "hot spots" where deeper nutrient-laden waters are brought to the surface by the physical process of "upwelling." In the nutrient-rich Antarctic waters alone (representing around 5 percent of the world's oceans), about 20 percent of the ocean production takes place. Such waters approach productivity levels of terrestrial forests, whereas most open oceanic waters exhibit production rates comparable to terrestrial deserts.

of solar radiation) the moisture factor determines in great measure the degree of potential production that is actually realized by terrestrial ecosystems. Highest production rates occur in wet forests, the lowest in arid deserts. Multiplying the production rate by percent of the earth's surface covered by the ecosystem type, one may obtain values for the percent of the world's annual production contributed by each ecosystem type.

Early calculations suggested that total production of the world oceans just about equals the total production of land ecosystems. Recent estimates based upon more complete data indicate that the oceans may be 10 to 15 percent more productive than previously supposed, but the earlier figure is retained in the present table for ease of comparison. Area for area, the world oceans on the average are about as productive as grasslands. The limiting factor in the marine environment is not moisture, however, but nutrient salts, particularly nitrates and phosphates. Although the deeper oceanic waters contain these salts in abundance, only the amount present in the upper 100 meters or so are important for primary production. Marine algae require both nutrient salts and radiant energy, and the latter is present only in the upper, lighted layers of the sea.

Primary production is not uniform throughout the marine environment. It is greatest in those areas where nutrient salts become highly available in the surface waters (i.e., near shore, in areas of deep-water upwelling, and in polar regions where the salt concentration is increased by freezing out of water crystals). In such areas the level of primary production may even approach that of the terrestrial forest.

Production by consumer species is known as *secondary production*. To understand this problem several factors must be considered. A number of consumer species often vie for the same food resource, but none of them actually "licks the platter clean." Some of the food organisms are generally left over, thereby allowing the food supply to keep coming on. It is frequently the case that much of the "potential" food supply is not really available to a given consumer species. The grasshopper cannot dig down and get at the plant roots, nor does it take the seeds, which are left for the mice and field sparrows; the spider rejects the grasshopper exoskeleton; the lion leaves bones, hide, and some flesh. Of the food material which is consumed, a portion is never assimilated into the body circulation but passes to the outside as fecal matter. Much of the assimilated material, in turn, is combusted to provide energy for the metabolic processes and is lost through respiration. Some of the unoxidized compounds are lost as urine. The small fraction which remains after all these losses is accumulated by the body as growth (or secondary production).

The ratio between growth and food supply available to produce the growth is referred to as the *gross efficiency* (which is usually expressed as a percentage). If 100 calories of pasture grass are required to produce 4 calories of growth in a cow, one can say that the cow has a gross efficiency of 4 percent. Studies of the efficiency of energy transfer among the consumer levels are still in their infancy, but already some generalizations seem justified. Within a given species gross efficiency values may vary rather widely in relation to such factors as developmental stage, type and quantity of the available food supply, general nutritional condition, stress, temperature, and so on. In effect, the animal must stay alive and well, and if there is anything left over after the maintenance tasks have been taken care of, it may then be used for growth.

Gross efficiency values currently available in the ecological literature range from about 4 to over 50 percent. Cold-blooded animals (*poikilotherms*) tend to exhibit higher efficiencies than warm-blooded forms (*homeotherms*), presumably because the latter use up a larger percentage of their food energy in the maintenance of an elevated body temperature. As a general rule of thumb one may think of consumer efficiencies as ranging around 10 percent (with 15 to 20 percent being closer for cold-blooded, and 5 to 7 percent being closer for warm-blooded animals).

With this background let us now examine the flow of calories through a portion of a grassland community of the United States (Figure 5.3). Although compiled from several sources, the figures are fairly realistic in light of what is currently known. Of the 470 million calories of radiant energy striking a square meter of grassland surface throughout a period of one year, only 6 million are "fixed" by the plants (for a net production efficiency of 1.3 percent). Of this 6 million potential food calories only 18,300 are converted into animal protoplasm by three (out of the many types) of primary consumer species. Obviously, if all the primary consumers had been included, this figure would be far higher. The grasshopper population alone produced 17,400 calories, which may be considered potential food for the spider population (secondary consumers). The spiders kill an amount equivalent to about 200 calories, of which, after all the various losses are accounted for, only 47 calories are converted into spider protoplasm.

In this grassland 10 million calories of sunlight produce only 1 calorie of spider! It will be recalled that on the average, producers are about 1 percent efficient but each consumer *level* is about 10 percent efficient. Thus, if all the consumers of each level had been included, the energy levels would appear as a set of stair steps proceeding from the high radiation level down to zero energy as shown in Figure 5.4.

In contrast with the biogeochemical cycles of nature, energy does not cycle. It passes through the system but once. At every transfer great quantities of energy are lost, so that in the end, when the last decomposer has oxidized the last organic molecule, there is complete dissipation of the original energy. After powering a complete carbon cycle, the energy origi-

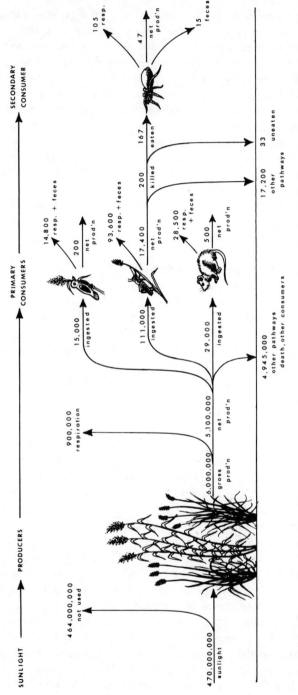

Figure 5.3. Generalized scheme of energy flow through a small portion of a grassland ecosystem. All figures are approximate and represent calories/square meter of surface area/year. Between 1 and 2 percent of the radiant energy received by the plants is used for carbon fixation (i.e., for gross production). Note that of the original 470 million calories falling upon the grassland only about 47 (i.e., one ten-millionth) wind up in the body of a single group of secondary consumers, the spiders. The progressive energy loss is considered to be the chief factor limiting the number of steps in the world's food chains. To achieve absolute maximum human population on the earth all people would have to eat plant rather than animal matter. Why? (Adapted from several sources.)

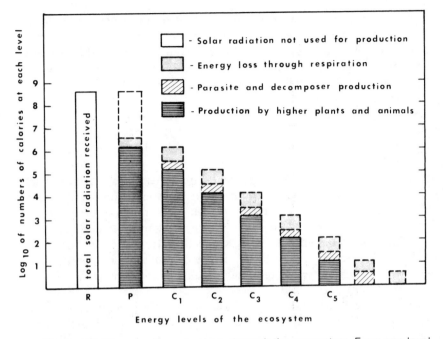

Figure 5.4. Stepwise flow of energy through the ecosystem. From one level to another, all the energy may theoretically be accounted for as either loss or production. Use of a logarithmic scale permits each category to be placed in approximately true proportion. *R* refers to solar radiation, *P* to producers, and *C* to consumers.

nally fixed through photosynthesis has been transferred completely to heat. Along the way the nitrogen, phosphorus, sulfur, and other biogenic elements have ridden their own separate courses through the system and are returned to their respective pools. Dust to dust.

Ecosystem Stability

Considering the diversity of the ecosystem components and the complexity of the pathways, it is a remarkable fact that the cycles of nature proceed in regular and orderly fashion. That they do so is fairly clear, but we do not yet understand exactly why. One can estimate the amount of each element present in the various pools and reservoirs and determine the rates of transfer from one to another. One can work out the pathways of energy transformation and estimate the flows through each pathway. But what regulates the system as a whole? What governs the overall rates of flow, apportions the elements and energy through the appropriate channels, and keeps the system quantitatively in balance?

In terrestrial systems the plants are controlled to some extent by available solar radiation, but they are limited primarily by the moisture factor and by those chemical nutrients of the soil which most closely approach the minimal (or maximal) limits of tolerance. For the most part, they are not controlled by the primary consumers (which take only a small fraction of the net production).

The major consumers, on the other hand, seem to be controlled from the top down. The highest carnivores control the next level down, and so on down to the herbivores. When external control fails, population will rise until internal mechanisms take over. It is a significant fact that in terrestrial ecosystems the top consumers are generally characterized by large size, great mobility, nutritional flexibility, and low reproductive rates. They can afford to "shop around" and seek food from any of the lower levels. If prey is unavailable in one area, they may move to another, even into a different ecosystem (as some do). In their turn, the top carnivores may be controlled in part by the available food supply and, in part, by their own territorial behavior (recalling that population density, rather than size, is the critical factor).

Decomposers are small, ubiquitous, and capable of very rapid reproduction. They are thus adapted for quick response to the nutritional opportunities occasioned by the wastes and corpses of the producers and larger consumers, whenever and wherever such opportunities may arise. In turn, they control the rate of inorganic nutrient release, and thus indirectly, the rate of primary production.

Such explanations as those given above are all undoubtedly true, in part, but they seem far too simple to account for the diversity of the ecological systems, and in any event, we do not have the hard quantitative data to assess them in detail. Many ecologists are now directing their efforts to the construction of mathematical models which simulate nature and at the same time account for system stability. Such models are being explored by a variety of computer techniques. Here again, the limitation is inadequate information about individual systems. Therefore, an intensive effort is currently underway by large teams of ecologists to provide the necessarily detailed information about a few of our major ecosystems (grassland, deciduous forest, fresh-water, and eventually marine). Much of this work is being sponsored by the International Biological Programme (IBP) whose theme is, "the biological basis of productivity and human welfare." Completion of these studies will take several years, but the ecosystem is a formidable system to unravel. The importance of these major studies in relation to our own welfare and survival will be considered in the next section.

Suggestions for Further Reading

BORMANN, F. H., and LIKENS, G. E. "The Nutrient Cycles of an Ecosystem." *Scientific American*, October 1970.

CHAPMAN, R. N. *Animal Ecology with Especial Reference to Insects.* New York: McGraw-Hill Book Co., Inc., 1931.

CLARKE, G. L. *Elements of Ecology.* New York: John Wiley & Sons, 1954.

COLE, L. C. "The Ecosphere." *Scientific American,* April 1958.

DEEVEY, E. S., Jr. "Mineral Cycles." *Scientific American,* September 1970.

EVANS, F. C. "Ecosystem as the Basic Unit in Ecology." *Science,* vol. 123, 1956.

GATES, D. M. "The Flow of Energy in the Biosphere." *Scientific American,* September 1971.

ODUM, E. P. *Fundamentals of Ecology.* Philadelphia: W. B. Saunders Co., 1971.

OOSTING, H. J. *The Study of Plant Communities.* San Francisco: W. H. Freeman & Co., 1956.

REDFIELD, A. C. "The Biological Control of Chemical Factors in the Environment." *American Scientist,* vol. 46, 1958.

SMITH, R. L. *Ecology and Field Biology.* New York: Harper & Row, Publishers, 1966.

ZOBELL, C. E. "Geochemical Aspects of the Microbial Modification of Carbon Compounds." In *Organic Geochemistry.* Oxford: Pergamon Press, 1963.

ZOBELL, C. E. "Organic Geochemistry of Sulfur." In *Organic Geochemistry.* Oxford: Pergamon Press, 1963.

synopsis

In the previous pages we have strolled through an unmolested garden of nature. We have dissected natural systems and studied the structure and function of the components. Before attempting to assess the role of man in relation to the natural systems, however, it is wise to review what has been said about the systems and to take a brief look at ecology itself.

The natural systems with which ecology deals are extremely diverse, i.e., they are composed of a great variety of functional parts. Each part is characterized by its own set of natural history peculiarities which simply represent adaptations to insure group survival in environments which are generally, if not always, predictable. For each of the components there is a series of built-in flexibilities so that the component may continue to exist and function even in the event of unusual stresses and strains.

At the present time we still do not understand the workings of a single component in *complete* detail, and it is unlikely that we ever will, so subtle and complex are the organism-environment and organism-organism relationships. In one recent study alone (dealing with the ecology and fishery of the salmon), about one thousand equations were employed. Nevertheless, with experience, common sense, and patient laboratory and field studies we may expect to learn the most significant facts about many of the components of the natural systems.

All ecological systems operate on some principle of dynamic balance. Their equations include numerators and denominators, both of which are subject to temporal variation. The observed levels are not static, but are the resultant of opposing forces which maintain the "steady-state" equilibria. A ready illustration is the population level in which the balance results primarily from the opposing forces of reproductive increase and environmental restriction. It is difficult to understand how the balance of opposing forces alone could account for all the equilibria of nature, however, and one is forced to conclude that the equilibrium levels basically represent inherently stable states roughly analogous to the stable states of the physical and chemical worlds. There is ample natural history justification for such a conclusion.

The integration of natural communities and ecosystems appears to be mediated largely by the flow of nutrients and energy through the biogeochemical and energy transfer pathways of food chains and food webs. The other communication systems of the community probably exert their main effects through their influence upon the nutritive pathways. The early-stage components of natural communities can either develop a new community from scratch or repair damage in the more mature communities.

The community-environment systems of nature, called ecosystems, are functionally independent of other such systems and are considered to be the really fundamental units of nature. Even though we may never completely understand all the working details of each ecosystem component, we already understand the ecosystem in a general way, and it is likely that we will achieve a better comprehension of the ecosystem as a whole than of all its component parts. This is due, in some measure, to the fact that the parts do not function the same when removed from the whole. It is also due to the fact that the parts may employ a series of subtle alternative methods to achieve the general goal of self-perpetuation within the framework of the self-perpetuating system.

All the ecosystems of the earth's surface are bound together in a very loose way through the gaseous biogeochemical cycles, and in particular, by the water and carbon cycles. All terrestrial ecosystems influence the fresh-water and marine ecosystems through the sedimentary cycles. This loosely-bound world system is known as the *biosphere.*

In overview the modern field of ecology represents man's effort to gain perspective on the grand systems of nature. As most fields of scientific endeavor become fractionated in their efforts to focus upon the smaller and smaller, ecology attempts to rejoin the disciplines to provide understanding of the larger and larger. Ecology also establishes a basis for the long view. On the grounds of what is known of the past and present systems, one can project down the road in general terms, and sometimes in specifics.

Because of the great complexity of the ecological systems, predictability rests in having access to adequate information about present and past correlations. Fishermen of the north Atlantic have learned that "white water" (that is, water rich in coccolithophores) is likely to produce good herring fishing, whereas water with a distinctive odor, called "backy juice"(due to the diatom *Rhizosolenia*) means poor fishing. For practical purposes one factor tends to be correlated with the other, even if the fishermen are not sure why. Correlation does not necessarily indicate causation, however. Year-to-year variation in codfish catches off the Norwegian coast are closely correlated with the annual growth rings of the Norwegian pine trees, but one is certainly not likely to be the cause of the other. Both, of course, reflect a third factor, weather, which determines tree growth, on the one hand, and local hydrographic conditions, on the other.

The ultimate factor in ecology is climate and its short-term local manifestation, weather. More accurate forecasting of weather conditions will surely lead to greater predictability of ecological phenomena. Satellite-based weather predictions, which have already begun aiding ecological studies, will surely become the basis for more accurate ecological predictions as their potential becomes realized.

II

man

and

nature

6. ecology

the relevant science

OECOLOGY

The science of domestic life. Biological economy.
Relations of the organism to the environment, and
to other organisms with which it lives.
Ernst Haeckel. 1869.

The *basic science of ecology*, rooted in the practical environmental knowledge of our distant ancestors and formally defined by Ernst Haeckel a century ago, seeks to understand laws governing the interrelationships of organisms with each other and with their nonliving environments. It is also the study of natural systems built upon such relationships. The first half of this book is devoted to this field, which we shall henceforth call "basic ecology."

Primitive man learned early that ecological knowledge could be employed to great advantage in furthering his own comfort, safety, and survival. Ancient artifacts and records attest to the gradual development of tools, clothing, housing, animal domestication, agriculture, irrigation, and the like, all means of achieving control over a seemingly hostile environment, and all based in some measure upon ecological knowledge. More recent development of crop rotation, contour plowing, forestry, game and fish management, economic entomology, and similar activities are but refinements of the earlier lessons. This area, the application of ecological knowledge to problems of human welfare, has long been known as the field of "applied ecology." Basic and applied ecology have coexisted quietly for many years.

Recently a third element has appeared on the scene with explosive force, blurring the differences between the two former fields and shaking the roots of society. If basic ecology deals with the relations of organisms with each other and with their environments, why should it not also include the human organism and its environmental relationships? In this view ecology becomes an umbrella uniting sociology, economics, public health, landscape architecture, urban and regional planning, sanitary engineering —

in fact, most fields of human endeavor. What, indeed, is now the distinction between basic and applied ecology if all of human society is involved? For present purposes we refer to this third area as "human ecology," and in the discussion which follows we will review some of the factors which have led to our sudden and dramatic awareness of this third area and its identification with ecology.

Historical Perspective

During the first half of the present century, scientists working in the areas of basic and applied ecology were aware of the similarities, differences, and interdependencies between their fields, and they labored quietly, each with his own research emphasis. Immediately before and after the Second World War, a group of ecologists was trained whose prime interest was the study of natural communities, for by then ecology had recognized that the total-system approach was within reach. Since the intent was to study basic ecology, examples of undisturbed nature were sought after. As early as 1950, the present writer, desiring to investigate the community ecology of an undisturbed stream, decided that the jungles of Latin America afforded the best possibility of locating a stream which had not, in some way, been influenced by human activity. The stream selected was largely virgin (as discussed in the Prologue), but even then and even there some human disturbance was noted. We were well aware of the Malthusian projections of human population increase and the problems which would be associated with overpopulation, but we had no way of foreseeing the compounding effect of recent technological development. A world economy geared to high production during the war was to accelerate many-fold in the years thereafter, and the atomic bomb which spread radioactivity over the surface of the planet ushered in a generation of environmental deterioration of unimagined proportions.

Later, in 1959, the author investigated another stream, this time in northern Illinois. Dr. Victor Shelford, often called the "father of animal ecology," had studied the stream in 1909, and from this work he had developed his theories of natural stream succession. Perhaps reinvestigation after a half-century interval would provide fresh insight into the stream succession problem. Examining the old collections of Shelford (and others) in the museums of the Chicago area, and revisiting the exact study sites, the author obtained, not a picture of natural succession, but a well-documented history of man's environmental irresponsibility. The fields and woodlands which early bordered the stream had given way to backyards. Stream flow, formerly rather regular, was now subject to violent fluctuation from rapid runoff. Cesspools openly dripped into the stream. Garbage, broken glass, old tires, cans, strands of wire, phonograph records, old newspapers, and other human waste abounded. The former clean-water community had almost vanished and was represented by a very small population in one deep ravine. In its place were found low density populations of hardy, garbage-tolerant forms, many of them nonnatives introduced by man. The introduced fishes included carp, goldfish, carp-goldfish hybrids, a bait minnow, and alewives from Lake Michigan. Of the few hardy survivors of the early group, some were clearly in poor physical condition.

The experience of this writer was paralleled by that of other ecologists, each working in this own area, and each time the answers were the same: human-induced environmental deterioration, loss of populations and natural communities, ecosystem destruction. As such reports appeared from ecologists working in the far corners of the world, the global magnitude of the problem began to take shape. Ecologists became more and more pessimistic, and realizing that they alone were witness to the demise of nature, many became frantic. At that time ecology had no platform through which it might bring the matter forcibly to the attention of the world and no "muscle" by which to effect the dramatic changes which would be necessary if nature were to be saved. The Ecological Society of America doggedly adhered to its policy of recognizing only basic research; there were no organized ecology lobbies in the state and federal legislatures; individual ecologists seldom had strong political ties; and ecological representation in the National Academy of Sciences was token, at best.

Historians tell us that new movements invariably come to prominence through unorthodox pathways, because the orthodox channels are already preempted by the ingroups. The period of the 1960s saw otherwise staid ecologists moving in a variety of unusual circles in a massive effort to get the message across where they felt it counted. These efforts, awkward, wavering, and disorganized at first, were catalyzed into a major movement largely by a single event, the appearance in the fall of 1962 of Rachel Carson's dramatic and thoroughly documented book, *Silent Spring.*

Throughout the late 1950s, solid scientific reports documenting the adverse effects of exotic chemicals upon wildlife were accumulating in the literature. Of especial note is the demonstration in 1957 that DDT and its chemical derivatives were accumulating in the waters of Clear Lake, California and were becoming magnified up the food chain so that the predatory diving birds which were dying off contained concentrations 100,-000 times that of the water itself. This was followed by the "cranberry scare" in which housewives throughout the nation refused to purchase cranberries known or suspected to be carrying high concentrations of a cancer-producing herbicide. Upon the heels of this came the discovery that a widely prescribed tranquilizer (thalidomide), when administered during pregnancy, often resulted in malformed human infants. Thus, by 1962 the general public and some government officials were becoming thoroughly alarmed over the potential dangers of widespread application and use of inadequately tested chemicals. They were ready to listen.

The message of *Silent Spring* was simple and forceful. Leveling its attack against chlorinated hydrocarbons, in general, and DDT, in particular, Miss Carson concluded that this "chemical barrage has been hurled against the fabric of life — a fabric on the one hand delicate and destructible, and on the other miraculously tough and resilient, and capable of striking back in unexpected ways." The field of applied entomology was ignoring basic ecology to the detriment of man himself. Even before it had appeared in print, the book was the center of intense controversy, and before the dust cleared several years later, Miss Carson's case had been adequately proven in several courts of law, most notably in the State of Wisconsin, where the issues and battle lines were most clearly drawn and where the decision was most clean-cut.

Details of the controversy are elegantly covered in Frank Graham's book *Since Silent Spring* (1970) and also in *Patient Earth* (1971) by Harte and Socolow, and they need not be reviewed here. What is most significant for present consideration is the fact that the environmental matter had now become a lively national and international concern. Ecologists, individually and collectively, were committed to a course of public action. Of especial importance was the decision of the Ecological Society of America to become involved. The Summary Report of the Ecology Study Committee, prepared by Dr. Richard S. Miller and transmitted on April 15, 1965, is quoted in part herewith, ". . . . Ecologists have a definite obligation to make their views known when they can provide information which might avert environmental problems that are properly within their area of competence. It is the feeling of the Ecology Study Committee that they should and must. It is obvious that if professional ecologists do not take initiative and provide responsible advice and leadership, less qualified and often irrational advice will be forthcoming from some other quarter." And again, ". . . . We are immediately faced with such problems as environmental pollution, population increase and control, resource development and management, and acquisition and management of public lands, but there is an even greater challenge to professional ecologists in the subtler principles underlying these questions. How, for example, are mineral and energy budgets and biological diversity affected by resource utilization? To what extent do industrial and agricultural development of specific environments affect homeostatic properties, and what homeostatic mechanisms are, in turn, brought into effect in such situations? As one member put it, 'Can we afford to preside over the gradual extinction of biological diversity?' Quite bluntly, profit is a driving force molding the ecosystems of man, but to what extent does a strict profit orientation have ecological survival? Our public responsibilities must be met, in other words, by demonstrating that ecosystem ecology can provide a perspective, stated as ecological forces, which are valuable in the solution of world problems."

Irrespective of the niceties separating basic and applied ecology, even the purest of the practitioners could no longer abdicate their responsibilities. They spoke out in classrooms, at public hearings, in legislative assemblies, on television, at ladies' groups, and in the pulpit. They wrote letters, editorials, articles, and books. They discussed environmental issues with political candidates and officials in public office. They beat pathways to gubernatorial offices and U.S. Senate chambers. They are still being heard, and they will not be denied by foot-dragging and political expediency. Chlorinated hydrocarbons are not the only agents through which man is destroying the natural world, and through nature, destroying himself. There are other cases to be made, and other battles to be won. The list is long and mostly familiar to us now: smog and other forms of air pollution, cultural eutrophication and other types of water pollution, resource depletion, genetic loss and species extinction, overpopulation and cultural degradation, etc. We are rapidly reducing the options of our children, and they have become acutely aware of the collective inertia of our generation and are resenting us for it.

Here and Now

Ecologists are no longer alone in possession of the knowledge of man's impact on the natural systems of the world. The basic case has been made, the news media quickly took note and spread the word, and by and large the citizens of this and several other advanced nations have heard and understood the real meaning of their warnings. A cab driver in Chicago apologizes to an ecologist for having to charge him a fare. A housewife, alarmed and confused, purchases only white toilet paper and puts a brick in the water tank of the toilet to conserve water. A ladies' group sponsors a drive to collect trash paper along the highway. A little girl asks plaintively, "Mommie, will I be allowed to have children when I grow up?" A U.S. Senator returning to Washington from a visit to Los Angeles turns to his colleague and says, "I have just seen the future, and it won't work!"

But what has actually been accomplished? With respect to pollution, what has been the response of government, the judiciary, industry, and the citizenry? Has population growth slowed down? Are resources being conserved? Do we yet have a firm scientific background upon which to base our environmental decisions? Let us examine the record.

During the past two years the tide has begun to turn. For whatever reasons — morality, ethics, fear, guilt, indignation — the attitudes of this and other nations have swung about, and progress has been made. There is now room for some cautious optimism. Perhaps it was the mercury crisis that brought the lesson home. The real danger of a can of poison tuna fish in the refrigerator may be more telling than all the spoken and published words.

Congress has moved effectively, passing a series of landmark bills, among the most important of which is the National Environmental Policy Act (Public Law 91-190) which went into effect January 1, 1970. This law reads, in part:

> . . . . (a) The Congress, recognizing the profound impact of man's activity on the interrelations of all components of the natural environment, particularly the profound influences of population growth, high density urbanization, industrial expansion, resource exploitation, and new and expanding technological advances and recognizing further the critical importance of restoring and maintaining environmental quality to the overall welfare and development of man, declares that it is the continuing policy of the Federal Government, in cooperation with State and local governments, and other concerned public and private organizations, to use all practicable means and measures, including financial and technical assistance, in a manner calculated to foster and promote the general welfare, to create and maintain conditions under which men and nature can exist in productive harmony, and fulfill the social, economic and other requirements of present and future generations of Americans.
>
> (b) In order to carry out the policy set forth in this Act, it is the continuing responsibility of the Federal Government to use all practicable means, consistent with other essential considerations of national policy, to improve and coordinate Federal plans, functions, programs and resources to the end that the Nation may—
>
> (1) fulfill the responsibilities of each generation as trustee of the environment for succeeding generations;
>
> (2) assure for all Americans safe, healthful, productive, and esthetically and culturally pleasing surroundings;
>
> (3) attain the widest range of beneficial uses of the environment without degradation, risk to health or safety, or other undesirable and unintended consequences;
>
> (4) preserve important historic, cultural, and natural aspects of our national heritage, and maintain, wherever possible, an environment which supports diversity and variety of individual choice;
>
> (5) achieve a balance between population and resource use which will permit high standards of living and a wide sharing of life's amenities; and
>
> (6) enhance the quality of renewable resources and approach the maximum attainable recycling of depletable resources.

(c) The Congress recognizes that each person should enjoy a healthful environment and that each person has a responsibility to contribute to the preservation and enhancement of the environment . . . .

The intent of this law is crystal clear. The Federal Government recognizes its environmental responsibility to the present and future generations, but it also charges the individual citizen to recognize his own personal responsibility. The same law proceeds to establish the Council on Environmental Quality (CEQ) and to spell out in detail the duties of this Council. It further charges all agencies of the Federal Government to employ a multidisciplinary approach to the solution of environmental problems and to cooperate fully with the Council.

Another important step by Congress is embodied in Public Law 91–438 which reads, in part:

. . . . (a) the Congress hereby finds and declares that the international biological program, . . . deals with one of the most crucial situations to face this or any other civilization—the immediate or near potential of mankind to damage, possibly beyond repair, the earth's ecological system on which all life depends. The Congress further finds and declares that the international biological program provides an immediate and effective means available of meeting the situation, through its stated objectives of increased study and research related to biological productivity and human welfare in a changing world environment . . . .
. . . . (c) In view of the urgency of the problem, the Congress finds and declares that the provision by the United States of adequate financial and other support for the international biological program is a matter of first priority . . . .

Curiously and unfortunately, many of the environmental bills passed by Congress have been ineffective due to the failure of the Bureau of the Budget to release appropriated funds. Although on shaky constitutional grounds, this freezing or impoundment of funds permits executive will to override the intent of the legislature by selective enforcement and funding. *Despite the smokescreen of rampant rhetoric, the only way the citizens of this country will ever achieve direct and apolitical progress toward the goal of environmental quality is to insure through the voting polls that the legislative and executive branches of government are of a single and progressive mind on environmental matters.*

Meanwhile, the newly created Environmental Protection Agency (EPA) of the U.S. Department of Commerce has been moving or threatening to move against certain of the most flagrant polluters among the municipalities and larger corporations. Some of the new laws have yet to be tested in the courts of the land, but the old Refuse Act of 1899 is an effective instrument if it is enforced vigorously.

Of late, the courts and the legal profession have been quite busy handling pollution suits. By and large the judiciary has familiarized itself with the field of ecology and the need for environmental protection, and it has recognized its own role as the weighing ground between economy and ecology. The environment is beginning to have its day in court. This is the ultimate anvil upon which tough environmental policy must be forged. The initial suits, requests for variances, denial of variances, court injunctions, fines, contempt suits, shutdown orders, the hearing of appeals — these are the stuff of which environmental protection is made, and the courts are now involved in hearing the evidence and making the decisions about the quality of tomorrow's world.

Among the plaintiffs are the federal, state, and local governments and certain private citizen's groups, of which the Environmental Defense Fund and Sierra Club have been most active and effective. Among the defendants have been the Secretaries of Agriculture and Interior, the Army Corps of Engineers, railroads and other corporate enterprises, state and local governments, and private property owners. The battle of the environment has begun, and it is being waged in the courts where knowledge and evidence are sacred and where truth and reason have a fighting chance.

Noise of the conflict also resounds in the state legislatures, city council meetings, citizens' study groups, and the news media, as well as in the rash of recent technical meetings and symposia. The spate of environmental books which have appeared in the past few years attests to the determination of indignant and vocal citizens of many walks of life. Ecology, the relevant science!

Suggestions for Further Reading

CARSON, R. *Silent Spring.* Boston: Houghton Mifflin Co., 1962.

COTTON, S. et al. *Earth Day — The beginning: A Guide for Survival.* New York: Arno Press, 1970.

Fortune eds. *The Environment: A National Mission for the Seventies.* New York: Harper & Row, Publishers, 1970.

GRAHAM, F. *Since Silent Spring.* Boston: Houghton Mifflin Co., 1970.

HARTE, J., and SOCOLOW, R. H. *Patient Earth.* New York: Holt, Rinehart, and Winston, 1971.

LOVE, G. A., and LOVE, R. M. *Ecological Crisis: Readings for Survival.* New York: Harcourt Brace Jovanovich, 1970.

MARINE, G. *America the Raped.* New York: The Hearst Corp., 1969.

OSBORN, F. *Our Plundered Planet.* New York: Pyramid Publications, Inc., 1968.

REINOW, R., and REINOW, L. T. *Moment in the Sun: A Report on the Deteriorating Quality of the American Environment.* New York: Ballantine Books, Inc., 1967.

RIDGEWAY, J. *The Politics of Ecology.* New York: E. P. Dutton, Inc., 1970.

SHEPARD, P. et al. *The Subversive Science: Essays Toward an Ecology of Man.* Boston: Houghton Mifflin Co., 1969.

7. people

The human population is a fabric woven of many threads. Life and death, childhood and adolescence, parenthood and old age, war and famine, riches and poverty, production and consumption, all are stitched together in the complex and variable patterns of the human tapestry. To understand this array and its environmental relationships we must first examine the warp and woof of population structure and the factors which together determine human numbers.

Demography

The census — The science of human numbers, *demography*, rests upon a broad and precise mathematical foundation. Given the number of individuals in the population at some starting time and allowing certain assumptions concerning the average behavior of individuals in the population, a demographer may readily compute the expected population size at any time thereafter. Conversely, given the size of the initial population and calculating what should happen under a variety of sets of alternative conditions, one can evaluate the assumptions if the actual population at subsequent time periods can be independently determined. Either way demographic analysis must rest ultimately upon some firm population figures, and these are derived primarily from the population census.

Originally designed to give simple numerical data, the census now provides for all manner of information concerning possessions and patterns of living, as well as human values and attitudes. Such information is valuable, not only in prediction of size and growth of the total population, but also to provide advanced estimates of geographic distribution, cultural requirements, and composition of the population and its subunits. Valuable predictive information is also derived from various types of polls and surveys, actuarial statistics, public health data, and hospital records. We are the most analyzed people in history and also the best understood.

Factors underlying population change — Demographic theory tells us that in a closed population (i.e., a population with no one entering or leaving) a stable population will tend to remain stable if births and deaths remain equal. Likewise, a changing population will, after a lag period, achieve stability if births and deaths come into balance. An excess of births over deaths results in population increase; the reverse leads to population decline. Of critical importance, therefore, is the birth-death ratio, often called the *coefficient of population change.* Since most human populations during historic time have been rising, the value is frequently referred to as the *coefficient of population increase.*

This coefficient itself is compounded from several sets of distinct but related factors which affect the numbers of individuals added to or subtracted from the population. These include such factors as the percentage of reproductive-age females in the population, percentage of females which become mothers, number of children per mother, average age at which children are produced (i.e., the mean generation time), and average length of life. Thus, factors which tend towards rapid population growth are high marriage rates, early marriages, large families, and long lives. Low population growth rates are associated with low marriage rates, late marriages, small families, and short lives. In addition to these factors which operate even in closed populations, the numbers of individuals can also change locally through patterns of human movement, i.e., through immigration and emigration.

Human vs. nonhuman populations — From the above considerations it is clear that numerical data for the mathematical analysis of human population changes are essentially the same as the information needed to calculate changes in plant and animal populations (given in Chapter 3). But there is a very important underlying difference. Plants and animals tend to reproduce seasonally throughout their reproductive lives according to set and predictable formulas. Within the limits of nutrition and population density, most lower forms reproduce to their maximum capabilities, and copulation takes place as if by random sexual encounter. Among the higher animals (especially birds and mammals), pairs may mate for a season or for life, but litter size is genetically determined. In nature the rules are set, and reproductive performance is highly predictable.

This is not the case in human populations. Humans are fertile all year long, mate selection is anything but random, and human control is (or can be) exercised over almost every one of the factors which enter the mathematical calculations. Abstinence from intercourse, contraception, deliberate abortion, family planning, balanced nutrition, public health protection (disease prevention), personal health protection (disease curing) are all deliberate human activities which are eventually reflected in population numbers. And behind each of these activities lies a set of culturally-derived values and attitudes based upon tradition, religious taboo, social pressure, and economic consideration, all however, modified by education and intellect. We differ from the creatures of the field by our actual or potential ability to control our own numerical destiny, and demographic analysis becomes a trivial exercise if it fails to take into account the changing values and attitudes which underlie the actual numbers.

Numbers of People

Precivilization — Man, or a close relative of man, has inhabited the earth for 2 - 2½ million years. By the time of the Neolithic Period (New Stone Age), about 8,000 B.C., he inhabited every continent except Antarctica, and he had mastered the manufacture of a sophisticated series of stone, bone, and wooden tools. Bows and arrows, spears and launching sticks were in wide use. Clothing was worn as necessitated by the climate, and body adornments were highly valued. Crude dwellings were constructed. The dog had long been a companion of man, and other animals and plants were undergoing domestication. Some human populations were nomadic and lived by hunting and gathering. Others were more settled and appreciated the rudiments of agriculture.

By analogy with what we know of existing primitive populations, we assume that the neolithic people reproduced early and frequently. Except in the most favorable environments, life was short, forty years being an exceptional age. Parasites, disease, accident, famine, and warfare combined to produce overall mortality rates nearly equal to the birth rates. Demographers estimate that by the Neolithic Period, the total world population had only reached a level of around 10 million humans.

Early civilization — The next eight millenia (i.e., the period from 8,000 B.C. to the time of Christ) witnessed great changes in the human way of life and marked the development of civilizations. Each arose in some particularly favorable environment, itself surrounded by an unfavorable buffer zone affording some protection from barbarian invasion. The fertile banks of the Nile, Tigris and Euphrates, Indus, Yangtze, and Yellow Rivers; peninsular Italy, Greece, Asia Minor, and India; islands such as Crete and Ceylon — these all cradled civilizations, each uniquely adapted to local conditions.

Development of sophisticated agriculture and intensification of domestication and herding permitted the growth of high-density settlements. Settlement led to cities, waterworks, and large-scale engineering. Local industry permitted craft specialization which produced high quality products of metal, glass, clay, wood, fiber, and other raw materials. The need for raw materials and markets for finished products led to expanding commercial horizons. Resulting governmental organization and class societies were stabilized by religion, ritual, and growing sets of traditions. In several instances high population and intense land use eventually exhausted local resources and ruined the land. Standing armies, originally developed to protect fields and flocks, were then employed for organized aggression as an extension of economic, political, and land-use policies.

In this period the lot of the average human in the civilized areas, at least, bettered considerably. Ways had been found to support high population densities through intensive land use, social specialization, and economic parasitism. The average length of life increased perceptibly. During these eighty centuries, from 8,000 B.C. to the time of Christ, the population of the earth increased twenty-five-fold, from around 10 million to about 250 million. Toward the end of this period (about 50 B.C.) Cicero summed up the prevailing practical philosophy concerning man's relations with nature (introduction to the present chapter).

Post-Renaissance — It is the year 1650 A.D. Oliver Cromwell has just established the British Commonwealth, and the Massachusetts Plymouth Colony is now thirty years old. Civilization long ago spread from its subtropical origins to new centers in the north temperate latitudes. Man has conquered the climate and the seas, and he has learned to live under governmental authority. Disease still abounds, and in 14-15 years London itself will be struck by the dreaded Black Plague (= bubonic plague: transmitted by fleas from rats to humans) which only three centuries before had killed about a third of the population of Europe. The western world, having awakened from centuries of ignorance and stagnation only yesterday, witnessed a rebirth of the arts, and tomorrow it will see practical men give rise to the age of reason. But right now the age of exploration has fostered a scramble for colonization. The major European powers have embarked upon a competitive adventure in world resource exploitation of unprecedented proportions. The "two-world" philosophy of "have" and "have-not" nations becomes firmly established. The year 1650 — world population has now risen to the half-billion mark.

Now it is 1850; two centuries have passed. America is a bustling independent nation, and the British Empire circles the globe. Western imperialism is near zenith. The industrial revolution cries for more resources, and technology devises ways of supplying them. Early marriages, large families, high infant mortality rates. The world population has now added its second half billion in only 200 years.

The year 1900. Science and medicine have begun to conquer the major dread diseases. Infant mortality decreases, and average life in the western world begins to lengthen dramatically. Another half-billion people have been added.

Science, medicine, public health, better nutrition. Another half-billion by the late twenties. Another by 1950. Miracle drugs. Another by 1960. Another by 1968. Only 8 years! Another by ... (Figure 7.1).

Population growth in a nutshell — World population growth may be expressed in several ways. We have seen that millions of years were required to add the first half-billion people but that only 8 years were required to add the last. There has been an unbelievable shortening of the time necessary to add a given number of humans. Another way of looking at the matter is to examine the doubling time. Beginning with the time of Christ, it took 1,650 years to double the population, but at the present rate of increase, it will take only about a third of a century. By the year 2,000, the world population should stand in excess of 7 billion, double the 1968 figure. Perhaps the most revealing statistic is given by the percentage rate of increase. It has been estimated that during the Paleolithic Period (Old Stone Age), a thousand years were required to add 2 percent to the world population. Now we are increasing at the rate of 2 percent a year! A thousandfold acceleration! Continuing at the present 2 percent per year rate, in the short space of 6½ centuries there will be one person for every square foot of land surface on the planet. Continuing for 15½ centuries, the total weight of people will equal the weight of the world — an absolute impossibility.

Conquest of death — The quickening pace of world population increase has been called, for good reason, the "population explosion." Its potential effect on the world's resources has, by analogy with the atomic and hydrogen bombs, been aptly called the "population bomb." What has led to the acceleration in numbers in recent years? The answer is easy to find.

Reviled by seventeenth-century witch hunts and the oppressive spirit of the Inquisition (in which church dogma stifled free intellectual pursuit), the libertarians of the eighteenth century firmly established the principles of both political and intellectual freedom. We hear Thomas Jefferson declare, "When I contemplate the immense advances in science and discoveries in the arts which have been made within the period of my life, I look forward with confidence to equal advances by the present generation and have no doubt they will consequently be as much wiser than we have been as we than our fathers were, and they than the burners of witches." Education was in high regard. Newspapers and books poured from the presses, and institutions of higher education sprang up like weeds in the older cities and along the expanding American frontier. Educators them-

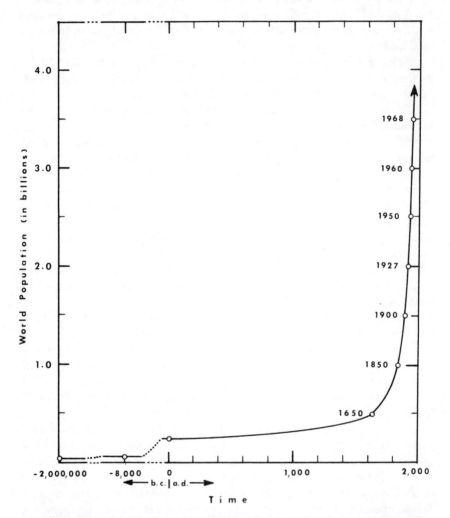

Figure 7.1. Growth in world population from the beginning of the human race up to the present time. The very early figures, of course, are simply educated guesses, but data for the past century or so are considered to be fairly accurate. Note the dramatic population increase in the past three centuries and the ominous shortening of the time required to add another half-billion people. While indicative of the overall situation, such generalized data do not reveal the desperate problems associated with local population concentration and the grossly unequal distribution of the resources among the world's people. (Adapted from several sources.)

selves were intellectually free to pursue both applied and theoretical research.

Of especial significance was the figure of Louis Pasteur, who in many ways dominated experimental biological science during the nineteenth century. Through his research investigations he was able to demonstrate that as a practical matter, life arises only from preexisting life. The opposite hypothesis (called "spontaneous generation") was experimentally untenable. Food spoilage does not naturally arise from food, and infectious disease does not spring *de novo* from a healthy body. Immediate practical results were the conquest of diseases of domestic animals (such as rabies) and of man (silk-worm disease and cholera). Medical antiseptics, surgical aseptics, disinfection, and the treatment and prevention of a variety of infectious diseases followed in short order. Pasteur also demonstrated ways of retarding the spoilage of milk (through pasteurization) and other foods. The world of nature is subtle, but not capricious. It is intelligible, and scientific experimentation can better the lot of man by conquering the age-old scourges of famine and disease.

The case had been forcefully made. An army of investigators entered the arena, and discovery piled upon discovery in medicine, agriculture, physics, chemistry and other fields of theoretical and applied science. In the western world mortality rates declined dramatically. Premature death, if not altogether conquered, was yielding rapidly. Hand in hand with the medical discoveries, agriculture developed means of increasing the yield per acre, as well as the yield per man-year of labor. Nutritional biochemists worked out the essential ingredients of a balanced human diet. Technology provided the power and gadgetry to free men from animal-type labor and brain-dulling drudgery.

In the industrial nations both the length of life and the quality of life has been increasing during the past century, but surprisingly the rate of birth has shown a sharp decline. It has in fact become axiomatic that all countries which have largely abandoned agriculture and which have become urbanized and highly literate have experienced marked declines in fertility rate. The reasons lie in the realm of education and attitudes; family planning; availability of birth control methods; recreational alternatives to intercourse; reduced need for children to provide support in old age; feeling of responsibility to provide better opportunities for the children which are produced; and the need or desire of adult women to seek employment, intellectual goals, or social roles beyond procreation and mothering. As a result, the western nations are now increasing by only 1 - 1½ percent per year. In the United States, for example, the birth rate at the moment only slightly exceeds the death rate, and were it not for immigration (which accounts for about 10 percent of our population increase), we would nearly have achieved zero-growth in this country, at least on a temporary basis.

Export of death-control methods — By contrast, the "developing nations" of Asia, Africa and Latin America are presently increasing by a factor of 3 - 3½ percent per annum, thanks largely to us. In the postwar period, we have widely exported the means of controlling death. Increased food-production methods aid in warding off starvation (which has been prevalent in many areas since prehistory). Improved personal health, environmental hygiene, and modern medicine coupled with public health have brought many of the endemic diseases under control. We have imposed twentieth-century death rates on populations still characterized by medieval birth rates in some of the most populous regions of the world, and the resulting social and environmental problems are enormous. These "have-not" nations have become acutely aware of the differences between their standards of living and ours, and they are striving against overwhelming odds to increase their own living standards. What is the effect of all this on the resources and environments of the world?

Environmental Impact of Population

Bringing the world up to our living standards — Let us suppose for the moment that the world population could remain stable with its present size and distribution for thirty years, during which time an all-out effort would be made to bring everyone's living standards up to our own. What level of resource use would be required? This can be approached in several ways, as follows:

1) The western world, which includes 14 percent of the world's population, enjoys about 56 percent of the world's income. At this rate one-fourteenth of the western world (representing 1 percent of the world population) receives 4 percent of the income. For all the world to share equally at this level, the world would have to produce 4 times its present income.

2) The United States, with 6 percent of the world's population, uses 40 percent of the world's resources and about a third of the world's power output. If all the people of the earth were to share our living standard, world resource utilization would have to increase to 667 percent and power production would have to rise to 555 percent of the present rate.

3) The average annual income for the world population (in dollar equivalents) is around $500 per person, but the comparable figure for the average American is about $3,000. For everyone to share our buying power, the world income would have to increase fivefold (actually, the income of the average African would have to increase nearly twenty-five times).

Regardless of the starting point, the figures come out about the same. A five- or sixfold increase in world production would be required just to bring the rest up to our rate of income and resource utilization — all this assuming the population remained steady. But the population will increase. In fact, it is going to double during the 30 year interval, and this would require, not a five- or sixfold but a ten- or twelvefold increase in production.

This is obviously not possible for several reasons. In the first place, the industrialized nations have spent years educating their citizens; training them to specialized tasks; building factories, houses, streets, highways, railroads, power lines, vehicles, and other necessities of advanced civilization. We have an accumulated store of capital investment which makes the high turnover rate both possible and profitable. In the second place, the U.S. gross national product (GNP) has increased steadily throughout the present century at a rate of about 3 percent per annum, i.e., faster than the population growth, thus allowing an average increase per person. The already overpopulated nations would have to increase their annual GNP outputs by 3 - 3½ percent just to stay even with their population rises and by at least 30 - 40 percent to catch up with us. If they were highly educated and already industrialized, there might be at least half a chance. But rampant poverty, inadequate diets, unskilled labor forces, widespread illiteracy, traditional social organization, and resistance to social change are all working against them. We cannot hope that natural fertility control, such as occurred in our case, will take over, because they cannot raise their own living standards fast enough to stay far ahead of the population increase. For them it has become a race for survival.

Feeding the world — Highly informed agricultural specialists tell us that, even at the projected rates of population increase, the world population can at least be fed during the next three decades. There are formidable problems of distribution, of making sure the diets are balanced, and of making the abundant and adequate food acceptable to starving people bound by strong traditions. Recent developments in farm mechanization, irrigation of arid lands, fertilization, and genetic manipulation of crop plants, together with the widespread use of chemical herbicides and insecticides have fostered a dramatic "green revolution." High-productivity strains of wheat and rice, as well as grasses for livestock, have been a great boon. Locally there are still great gaps between production and consumption, and often the progress has been least where it is most needed, but it looks as if the people can be fed. But at what price?

High production requires both intensive and extensive land use. The native terrestrial ecosystems of the planet are dwindling at an alarming rate to make more land to support more people. The herbicides, insecticides, and fertilizers are eliminating the ecosystems of our lakes and streams and are severely damaging the marine life. Shrimp along the Latin American coast are already so highly charged with chlorinated hydrocarbon pesticides

that their consumption constitutes a human health hazard. Shall we feed
the polluted marine products to our pets and our livestock? Some very
serious questions must soon be faced. Can the earth survive without its
native ecosystems? If we feed man from the land, can we also expect any
significant and useful harvest from the sea? How long can technology keep
us at least even with population?

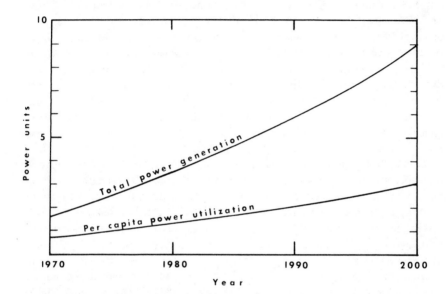

Figure 7.2. Projected growth in power generation and estimated *per capita*
power utilization in the United States through the year 2,000. Total power
generation is expressed in trillions of kilowatt-hours per year, and *per capita*
utilization is expressed in ten thousands of kilowatt-hours per year. By the
year 2,000 nuclear energy should be supplying substantially over half the
power requirements of society. Note that the *per capita* power utilization
will more than triple during the 30-year period. (Data on projected total
power generation derived from Krenkel and Parker, 1969. Estimated *per
capita* power generation obtained by dividing projected population sizes
into estimated total power generation.)

Population impact on material resources of the world — We have seen in
Chapter 3 that unrestrained population increases at a logarithmic rate, as
indicated by the notation, e^{rt}, where the exponent r represents the time-
related increase factor. In the present chapter we have noted that a rise
in civilization is accompanied by a greater *per capita* increase in power utilization, material goods, and wealth. To provide these increased commodi-

ties and services requires a greater per-person utilization of the world's resources, and this factor is also increasing at a logarithmic rate. We may use the notation, e^{it}, where the term i reflects the time-related environmental impact of the average person in the population. The environmental impact of the total population becomes the product of these two factors; thus: $e^{it} \times e^{rt} = e^{(i+r)t}$. This is the real message of the present chapter, the compounding effect of per capita-times-population impact. A few examples will illustrate the point.

In 1950 the average person in the world required the energy equivalent of one ton of coal. By the year 2000 the average person will require the equivalent of about 3 tons of coal. During this period the world population will have grown from 2.5 to 7 billion, almost a threefold increase, but the power requirements will have increased roughly nine times. (Actually, the average American already uses the equivalent of approximately 50 tons of coal, and the per capita use is increasing [Figure 7.2]).

We have been referring to the world's resources as though all were present and available in limitless supplies, but such is certainly not the case. At their present projected usage rates, the remaining economically exploitable reserves of such metals as copper, lead, tin, and zinc should last only about 20–35 years. Recycling will, of course, extend the life of the reserves, and when something gets in really short supply, we may have to tap some of the available resources which are uneconomical at present. However, the energy required to obtain these treasures, for example, the metals dissolved in seawater, will really be astronomical. The main point here is that significantly raising the standards of living of the underdeveloped nations would require the extensive use of specific raw materials which are already in very short supply. Just to provide the copper for the necessary electric power transmission lines would be prohibitive. For some of the projected world material needs, attention is called to Table 7.1, and the reader is invited to read McHale's recent and stirring book, *The Ecological Context*, which documents these needs in great detail.

Conclusion — The rising hopes of three-fifths of the world's population cannot conceivably be met within the context of the known world resources. We can keep these humans alive for a few generations, but the discrepancy in material wealth between the "haves" and "have nots" will continue to grow as the numerical superiority of the "have nots" continues to rise. This double polarization forebodes great social and political instability in the years immediately ahead, and the systems of nature, already shrinking and overtaxed, will be subject to greatly intensified pressures. The matters of birth control and resource sharing must replace ideology and competition in the minds of national and international leaders if long-range human survival is considered a worthy goal.

TABLE 7.1

YEAR World Population (billions)	1970 3.7	1980 4.6	1990 5.7	2000 7.0
METALS				
Iron	560.0	900.0	1400.0	2250.0
Aluminum	11.3	32.0	90.0	250.0
Copper	6.2	9.2	13.5	20.0
Zinc	5.0	7.2	10.4	15.0
Total	582.0	948.0	1514.0	2535.0
SYNTHETICS				
Plastics	27.0	105.0	420.0	1700.0
Synthetic rubbers	5.5	11.5	23.0	44.0
Man-made fibers	7.2	13.0	24.5	46.0
Total	40.0	130.0	467.0	1790.0
NATURAL PRODUCTS				
Natural rubber	2.5	2.6	2.8	3.0
Natural fibers	21.5	30.2	41.5	60.0
Total	24.0	32.8	44.3	63.0
Total requirements	646.0	1,111.0	2,025.0	4,388.0*

*Note: 4388.0 million tons of materials would occupy a volume of over 2 billion cubic meters (as it will when it becomes waste).

Material requirements of present and projected world populations expressed in millions of tons of materials. (Adapted from R. Houwink, The Synthetics Age In: *Modern Plastics,* vol. 43, issue 12, pp. 98-100, McGraw-Hill, Inc., August, 1966).

Suggestions for Further Reading

Boerma, A. H. "A World Agricultural Plan." *Scientific American,* August 1970.
Cloud, P. *Resources and Man.* San Francisco: W. H. Freeman & Co., 1969.
U.S., Congress, House, Subcommittee of the Committee on Government Operations. *Effects of Population Growth on Natural Resources and the Environment.* 91st Cong., 1969.
Ehrlich, P. R. *The Population Bomb.* New York: Ballantine Books, 1968.
Ehrlich, P. R., and Ehrlich, A. H. *Population, Resources, Environment: Issues in Human Ecology.* San Francisco: W. H. Freeman & Co., 1970.

HARDIN, G. *Population, Evolution, and Birth Control: A Collage of Controversial Ideas.* San Francisco: W. H. Freeman & Co., 1969.

HARRER, J. G. *Prospects of the World Food Supply: A Symposium.* Washington, D.C.: National Academy of Sciences, 1966.

HAUSER, P. M. et al. *The Population Dilemma.* Englewood Cliffs, N. J.: Prentice - Hall, Inc., 1969.

KEYFITZ, N., and FLIEGER, W. *Population Facts and Methods of Demography.* San Francisco: W. H. Freeman & Co., 1971.

KRENKEL, P. A., and PARKER, F. L. *Biological Aspects of Thermal Pollution.* Nashville: Vanderbilt University Press, 1969.

McHALE, J. *The Ecological Context.* London: Studio Vista, 1971.

SCRIMSHAW, N. S. "Food." *Scientific American,* September 1963.

THOMAS, W. L. et al. *Man's Role in Changing the Face of the Earth.* Chicago: University of Chicago Press, 1956.

8. environmental

pollution

The Dilemma of an Estuarine Fish

A few miles offshore in the Gulf of Mexico, a young fish completes its embryonic development and begins to swim. This is an Atlantic croaker, important forage fish, and for man a food and game species. Its life history calls for this fish to migrate shoreward and to enter a low salinity estuary where food and shelter are abundant and where predators are relatively few. Feeding and growing in the estuarine nursery grounds, the fish should eventually achieve adult size and become sexually mature. Then it must retrace its path and move back out to the ancestral spawning grounds in the offshore waters to reproduce, thus continuing the annual cycle, unbroken through countless generations.

To carry out its migration the little fish must move several miles, hitching rides on the incoming tidal currents and guided along its path by subtle estuarine odors, salinity gradients, and bottom water currents. Through eons of evolutionary time, the fish's ancestors have become genetically adjusted to reproduce at the place where the migratory signals are just right, at the season when the currents are favorable for the trip, and when food is most plentiful for the critical early stages of growth. The natural odds against the young fish are great, but enough individuals must be able to complete the hazardous cycle to perpetuate the species population (Figure 8.1).

This year things are different. Engineers, trained in hydraulics, construction, and cost-benefit ratios, have built dams which retain the fresh water in the upstream reaches of the river. Bottom currents are not like

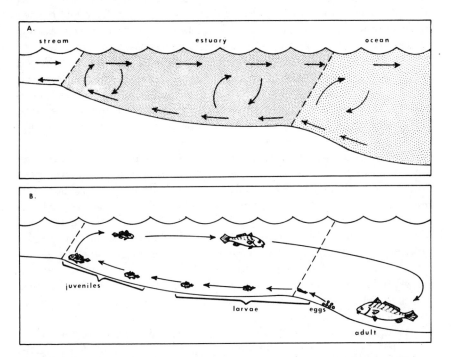

Figure 8.1. Role of the estuary in the life cycle of a typical coastal fish species. A. Generalized pattern of water circulation in the estuary. Fresh water is generally less dense than the relatively salty water of the estuary, and it tends to move seaward at the surface. Ocean water is saltier and denser, and it tends to creep upstream along the bottom. This pattern of vertical stratification is especially pronounced during the summer months when temperature reinforces the salinity-based density differences. Wind action may induce vertical mixing, thereby temporarily breaking down the pattern of vertical stratification. B. Life cycle of a fish species as illustrated by the Atlantic croaker (*Micropogon undulatus*). Eggs are laid in the sea but not far from the passes. Larvae migrate into the estuaries aided by the bottom currents. Most feeding and growth takes place in the estuaries. When mature, the adults move again to the outside waters. Most of the world's commercially important species of fishes, shrimps, and crabs exhibit life history patterns which deviate from that of the croaker only in minor details. Thus, if the world's marine fishery harvest is to be maintained efforts must be made to preserve the integrity of the estuaries. This problem is especially crucial in the developing nations which absolutely depend upon protein from the sea. (Adapted from Cronin and Mansuetti, in: Douglas, P.A. and R.H. Stroud, *A Symposium on the Biological Significance of Estuaries,* Washington, D.C.: Sport Fishing Institute, 1971, pp. 20 and 34.)

they have been before. The subtle odors of the natural estuarine water are now masked by a thousand exotic chemicals which have entered the stream through the activities of streamside farmers and manufacturers and by city sewage disposal plants. The tiny crustaceans upon which the fish normally feeds have been greatly reduced by pesticides, aimed at insects but also lethal for crabs, shrimp, and other insect relatives. Food is scarce, and that which is found and consumed is charged with exotic chemicals which, in turn, reduce the vitality of the little fish. With the journey thus slowed and the residence time in the offshore waters lengthened, vulnerability to predation is correspondingly increased.

If the fish does eventually make it into the estuary, he may encounter abnormally high salinity conditions. The normal river flow has been checked by the dam, its fresh water being diverted for irrigation, industrial, and municipal use. As a result of the higher salinity, marine predators are in greater evidence, even in the former haven of the estuary. Food is scarcer than usual because the dam which impounds the water also holds back the silt and organic matter which formerly fertilized the estuary. Furthermore, many of the marshes and mud flats no longer support the luxurious plant and bacterial growths upon which the fish used to feed; instead they are now surrounded by concrete walls and filled in for housing developments and boat marinas.

Within the water itself, and especially in the bottom sediments, are found heavy concentrations of herbicides, pesticides, and other organic chemicals as well as several heavy metals including lead, mercury, and cadmium. The same basic factors which cause nutrients to be retained within the estuaries also result in the entrapment and concentration of the noxious nonnutritive chemicals. In high concentration many of these chemicals can kill outright, whereas at lower levels they induce stress, sickness, and metabolic interference.

From time to time the local power plant (which produces electrical energy for industry and the municipality) releases "slugs" of hot water into the estuary because the estuarine water must be used to cool the condenser coils. If not killed outright by the heated water, the fish is placed under great stress. The elevated water temperature increases the fish's metabolic rate and its need for oxygen while simultaneously reducing the oxygen supply available; it increases the fish's food and energy requirements at a time when it is killing the food supply; it increases the fish's sensitivity to the chemical poisons at a time when the fish is already under stress from heat, low oxygen, and malnutrition.

If, by chance, the fish does survive the natural and artificial hazards of the estuary and is able to arrive successfully at the spawning grounds, the dangers are still not past. The eggs produced may be so loaded with toxic chemicals that many are unable to develop into normal young. Those which do complete their embryonic development begin life with a heavy chemical burden which further reduces their chances of fulfilling the normal life history pattern. Year after year, generation after generation, civilization adds burden upon load, stress upon strain, which in total, poses a many-horned dilemma in the fish's struggle to survive.

Nor is the case of the Atlantic croaker an isolated example. Two score years ago, the writer journeyed to the tropical jungles to study an unpolluted stream. Even then the ecologist was aware of the gradual demise of nature. Now, however, it is impossible to find a stream, lake, estuary, ocean, or land area on the entire earth that does not show evidence of some form of human pollution. Birds are dying out in Bermuda, presumably from DDT accumulation, though DDT usage has long been prohibited in the islands. Deep-water crabs in Antarctica contain measurable amounts of DDT, but DDT is not used in quantity within thousands of miles of the southern continent. Tunafish of both Atlantic and Pacific Oceans display high quantities of mercury, but tunas do not feed near land or estuaries. Even the frozen Arctic is about to witness oil spillage which will surely ravage wide acreage, if on land, or vast marine areas, if in water. And, of course, man-made radioactivity may be detected throughout all ecosystems.

Ecological Principles Related to Environmental Pollution

The complex nature of the environmental pollution problem has been illustrated by a specific case in order to provide the reader with some insight into the interaction of pollutants with natural ecological factors and to demonstrate that many of the most important effects of pollution are quite subtle and visible only to the specialist who knows the species and who is able to study and interpret the various life history and ecosystem functions. A few examples have been given to demonstrate that the case of the croaker is not an isolated instance, but that the pollution problem has become a menace of global proportions. With this background we may now define pollution, as the ecologist sees it, and examine certain general concepts or ecological principles which have rather universal application to pollution problems.

1. *A pollutant may be defined as any agent which when added to the environment by man creates stress beyond that which would have been occasioned by natural forces alone.* Pollution is the extra load placed upon the individual, population, or ecosystem, and it is comparable to the burden of taxes and surtaxes observed in human economic systems. Pollution is the price which nature pays to support high human population and high civilization.

Under normal environmental conditions, living systems of nature are fairly well adjusted to their environments, and most can withstand *moderate* additional pressure. Indeed, when moderate pressures are relaxed, living systems can generally be expected to recuperate, reestablishing the former balance within a short time. But natural environments are themselves subject to occasional extreme conditions, and even moderate additional pressure may become unbearable if applied during critical periods. Heated effluent from a power plant may cause little damage to a stream or estuary during the cooler months, but it may prove disastrous during midsummer when the aquatic organisms are already struggling to survive at or near their maximum limits of thermal tolerance.

Heavy unidirectional stress of long duration tends to eliminate the recovery mechanisms so that the capability for complete recuperation is lost. Even if the pressure is eventually relaxed or removed altogether, the heavily stressed system, although it may regain some integrity, never again achieves its former level. This phenomenon has not been widely recognized because many cases are known where heavily polluted areas have been cleaned up and repopulated. A good example is the partial recovery of the lower Thames River following pollution abatement. In every case, however, the restored populations must reinvade from some external refuge, and the new system is distinct from the previous one, which is lost forever. The reader must here ask himself what will happen when there are no more refuges, because that is the singular prospect which is now driving many practicing ecologists into political and literary ventures. No more refuges!

2. *For practical purposes two general classes of polluting agents may be recognized: those which are potentially harmful at any but trace amounts* (gradual agents) *and those which become deleterious only at higher concentrations* (threshold agents) (Figure 8.2). In the first category one recognizes several types of radiation, a number of heavy metals, and a great variety of industrial and agricultural chemicals. Radiation and heavy metals have long been present at low levels in most natural environments, and through evolutionary time, organisms have become adjusted to handling these small background amounts with minimal damage.

The problem now faced by countless millions of organisms, and indeed by large segments of the world ecosystems, is the sudden and simultaneous flood of exposure to a diversity of these potentially damaging factors. Many of the radioactive materials, hazardous metals, and exotic chemicals tend to remain in the environment and to accumulate so that year after year the load builds up. Evolutionary adaptation to background levels took place through countless millions of years, and there is simply not enough time available for the organisms to develop genetic adjustments to the diversified and increasing loads which are now being imposed. As the pressure mounts, the inevitable result is the selective elimination of the most sensitive individuals, populations, and eventually ecosystems.

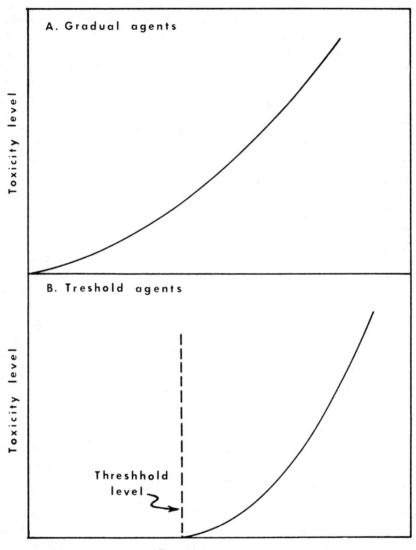

Figure 8.2. Toxicity-dosage relationships of the two general classes of polluting agents. A. Gradual agents. In this case toxicity is proportional to dosage at all but trace levels. B. Threshold agents. The organism or system is able to handle a certain amount of the pollutant seemingly without ill effect, and toxicity symptoms begin to appear only after a certain threshold level has been achieved.

The *threshold agents* include heat, the various elements of fertility, and organic wastes, all of which tend to stimulate biological development when applied in small or moderate amounts. When provided in excess quantity, however, the living systems may become overstimulated, and some processes proceed too fast for the regulatory mechanisms to keep the systems in balance. This results in considerable modification in the functional components, often followed by general collapse of the system.

Tragic examples of the overstimulation phenomenon may be found in many of our lakes, streams, and estuaries which have been enriched with fertilizer (through runoff from heavily fertilized farm fields), detergents and domestic sewage (from municipalities), or organic wastes (from poultry operations, meat processing plants, and other organic industries). Excess fertilizer stimulates the growth of aquatic plants, including both the microscopic algae and the larger rooted vegetation. The plants eventually die and undergo bacterial decomposition. If the load is already organic (sewage, chicken guts, beef trimmings, etc.) the vegetation step is bypassed, and the material itself may decompose directly. In either event the bacteria require a great deal of oxygen to burn the extra load of fuel, and if the rate of decomposition exceeds the rate of oxygen replacement, the system becomes anaerobic. But long before the last molecule of oxygen has been used up, all of the higher animals and most of the plants have disappeared. This has now become a community of decomposer organisms (bacteria, molds, protozoans, and sewage worms). The phenomenon of overenrichment, technically referred to as *cultural eutrophication,* is of widespread occurrence in shallow waters throughout the civilized world.

3. *An organism's sensitivity to a given polluting agent tends to vary with life history stage and with metabolic condition.* For most animal species the juvenile forms are more sensitive to and less capable of avoiding environmental pollutants than are adults. Chlorinated hydrocarbons and heavy metals are especially severe on immature animals, but excessive heat, radiation, and other stress agents also tend to affect the young first.

Let us illustrate this with an example from human populations. In the towns of Minamata and Niigata on the coast of Japan, postwar industrial plants manufacturing a chemical (acetanilide) found it convenient to dump mercury-containing wastes into the neighboring bays from which the local populations regularly harvested fish, shellfish, and other dietary staples. In Minamata alone, between 1953 and 1960, 111 cases of severe mercury poisoning were detected. Forty-three persons died, and the remainder showed a variety of neurological symptoms including insanity, paralysis, blindness, and locomotor and speech impairment. Mercury easily passes the placental barrier, and the high frequency of congenital defects in normal or near-normal mothers demonstrates the sensitivity of the unborn. The important point which must be made in this connection is that government standards for the release of potentially toxic chemicals must take into account the most sensitive stages of an animal's life history. In humans this generally means safeguarding the developing foetus (recall the thalidomide episode), but it also means protecting the mother who is undergoing the stresses of pregnancy.

In the case of plants, the seeds tend to be quite resistant to environmental extremes, and the larger plants are more sensitive to damage from ionizing radiation and other damaging agents than are younger and smaller members of the same species. Larger plants expose more surface area to damaging radiation, but the detailed reasons for adult-sensitivity are not well understood.

Organisms already under stress from illness, parasites, or fatigue are clearly more sensitive to the effects of polluting agents than are healthy, fresh individuals. Pollution stress added to an already weakened metabolism may pose an intolerable burden upon a plant or animal which would otherwise possess the stamina to take it. Consider the case of the migratory bird which has stored large quantities of DDT and other chlorinated hydrocarbons "safely" in its fat deposits. During the long, strenuous migratory journey, the bird burns the fat to fuel the flight. As the fat supply becomes exhausted, the bird literally loads its system with the hydrocarbons. In this case the metabolic condition of the bird determines the actual chemical load to which the individual is subjected, and the "safe" load now becomes lethal.

4. *Two or more polluting agents acting simultaneously may exert a combined effect different from the simple sum of the factors acting independently.* In some instances the pollutants do behave in simple-sum fashion, especially at low levels of exposure, but as a general rule this is not the case. Sometimes one agent tends to partially cancel the action of another (*antagonistic* effect), but more often the combined effect is more severe than the sum of the two acting separately (*synergistic* effect).

Amelioration is not considered to be common, but some examples are known, and others are suspected. For example, potassium cyanide is a deadly compound which blocks respiration in most aquatic animals. As an industrial byproduct it has long been dumped into the Houston ship channel (and other "industrial" waterways). Acids dumped into the channel in quantity by other companies convert the potassium cyanide into hydrogen cyanide gas which then escapes into the atmosphere. This would reduce the toxicity of the cyanide for fishes and other aquatic animals (if they were able to tolerate the other pollutants in the channel, which they cannot).

Examples of synergistic action, on the other hand, are rampant. Elevated temperatures greatly increase the sensitivity of many fishes to the effects of pesticides and heavy metals, even though the temperatures themselves are still well within the normal range of tolerance. Chlorinated hydrocarbons, known to be toxic to many marine organisms tend to be relatively insoluble in seawater. The solubility can be increased manyfold if other hydrocarbons are present (as from an oil spill), and the solubility is further enhanced if detergent is added (to disperse the oil spill). Considering the fact that man now manufactures several hundred thousand different chemical compounds and that many of these find their way into the environment in quantity, the opportunities for synergistic action are astronomical.

5. *The concentration and environmental distribution of a given pollutant is determined by the combined effect of a series of factors which, in the case of most pollutants, are poorly known at present.* In elementary terms the environmental concentration of a given substance reflects the equilibrium between rate of release and rate of removal. For many agents man is simply adding to the levels already resulting from natural processes such as the natural erosion of mercury from rocks containing cinnabar and other mercuric compounds. For other agents, including many industrial compounds, there is no known natural counterpart, and man is the sole producer.

Upon entering the environment through one of the industrial, agricultural, or domestic channels, each pollutant embarks upon its own specific biogeochemical adventure, the characteristics of which are determined, in part, by the chemical and physical nature of the pollutant and, in part, by the environmental circumstances encountered along the way. Recall that cyanide will remain in the aquatic medium if the water is alkaline, but that acidic conditions drive it into the atmosphere.

As pollutants come into contact with one another and with natural environmental agents, they may react to form secondary, tertiary, quarternary, etc. products. For example, urban atmospheres are constantly being "enriched" with a variety of substances which through a series of steps results in the production of a dangerous gas called *ozone* capable of causing considerable lung damage. This, in turn, may react with a series of other chemicals to form *peroxyacyl nitrate* (PAN), a compound which irritates mucous membranes, especially the eyes. Sunlight, moisture, gases, and particles react in various and poorly understood ways to produce a series of other chemicals which eventually enter the soil and waters of the earth, and what happens thereafter can often only be guessed at.

During its period of residence in the atmosphere and in the water, a pollutant may be transported by currents many miles from the original site of injection. A nuclear blast in China is followed by a rain of radioactivity in North America. Antarctic penguins contain measurable amounts of DDT even though most DDT usage occurs north of the equator, and none is used within many miles of the southern continent.

Eventually most pollutants leave the active circulation of the biosphere through change in chemical or physical form or through burial. For many, the marine sediments form the ultimate sink. The length of time a given pollutant is in active circulation is an important factor in determining its opportunities for accumulating and damaging living systems.

But the living systems themselves are not without effect upon the pollutants. For many years it was thought that metallic mercury when released into the aquatic environment simply became buried in the sediments where it was thereafter out of circulation. We now know that clams and other bottom dwelling animals pump materials from below back to the surface sediments and that bacteria are capable of transforming mercury from the inorganic to soluble organic forms. Through these biological processes the mercury is able to pass from the sediments into the water column and also to enter the biological food chains.

In some cases the organisms modify the toxicity of a pollutant. The organo-mercury compounds mentioned above are generally more toxic than the metallic mercury itself. DDT is eventually broken down to nontoxic residues, but along the way it may be converted to the more toxic DDE form. Petroleum residues, many of which are highly injurious to aquatic life, are eventually detoxified by bacteria.

Perhaps the most striking example of biological modification of pollutants is exhibited in the phenomenon of *"magnification."* Reference was made earlier to the Clear Lake tragedy in which DDT accumulated up through the food chains so that the predatory diving birds reached concentrations 100,000 times that of the water itself. The same phenomenon has now been amply documented from Lake Michigan (Figure 8.3) and many other aquatic and terrestrial areas. It has now become something of a general rule that the highest predators in natural food webs are the ones most likely to exhibit the highest concentrations of polluting agents. The list of predatory birds endangered by pesticides grows daily. Among marine fishes the mercury concentration tends to be highest in the predatory species: swordfish, tunas, barracudas, groupers, etc. Carnivorous human populations, such as the Eskimos, which occupy the apex of some food pyramids may themselves become the greatest concentrators of all.

6. *Biological response to pollution stress takes two forms, specific and generalized, and both types of response are observable at every level of biological organization.* Much has already been said about specific biological responses to particular polluting agents, and this point need not be belabored further. Nor is it necessary to repeat the earlier discussions (see Chapters 1 and 3) of the generalized responses of individual organisms and populations to environmental stress. What remains is a discussion of the generalized responses of communities and ecosystems to stress situations.

During the past two decades, a great deal of study has been devoted to the effects of ionizing radiation on terrestrial communities, a situation in which response may be related quantitatively to dosage. In summary, these studies demonstrate that with increasing exposure there is a progressive dissection of the structure of the forest, layer by layer. The pines drop out, then the oaks, followed in order by the taller shrubs, the lower shrubs, and the herbs. The last to go are the low mosses and lichens. Within a given stratum the most sensitive species are the specialists, and the most resistant are the generalists, the everyday weeds which tolerate all manner of disturbance. Associated with these changes in species composition are progressive reduction in total standing crop, reduction in species diversity, decrease in stability, and changes in the ratio of photosynthesis to respiration. Of great importance is the shift from tight nutrient cycles to open ones with considerable loss of nutrients from the system. With reduction of the plant cover, erosion removes nutrients from the ground and temporarily overenriches the streams. But the land progressively loses its potential for recovery. Reduction and loss of vegetation and nutrients is accompanied by progressive failure of the animal communities (Figure 8.4). These changes, amply documented in radiation studies, are closely paralleled by community responses to other forms of environmental pollution.

Only a little reflection is necessary to realize that the effects of progressive pollution are essentially the reverse of the natural biological processes of succession and evolution. Man has reversed nature! As succession and evolution have led to complexity, balance, and life support, pollution inexorably induces simplicity, imbalance, and reduction of ability to support life. The fine genetic adaptations, developed through countless millions of years of trial-and-error experiments, are being swept out of existence in one human generation.

Whether dealing with individual organisms, populations, or communities and ecosystems, the specialist can readily recognize the general symp-

Figure 8.3. Ecological magnification of a chlorinated hydrocarbon pesticide ▶ (DDT and its derivatives) in the Lake Michigan ecosystem. From an initial concentration of 0.003 parts per million in the sediments through the crustaceans and fishes, to the final concentration of 80 ppm in the herring gulls, the pesticide has become magnified by a factor of 27,000 This body burden interferes with the calcium metabolism of the bird and results, among other things, in the production of eggs with very thin shells. Most of these eggs break during the normal course of incubation, and consequent reproductive failure presently threatens the continued existence of many species of birds which occupy the upper levels of food chains. (This figure is based upon data given by Joseph J. Hickey and quoted by Orie L. Loucks in *Patient Earth*, ed. by J. Harte and R. H. Socolow, 1971.)

80 ppm

(27,000x)

1.8 – 2.3 ppm

(600 – 800x)

(70 – 100x)

0.2 – 0.3 ppm

0.003 ppm

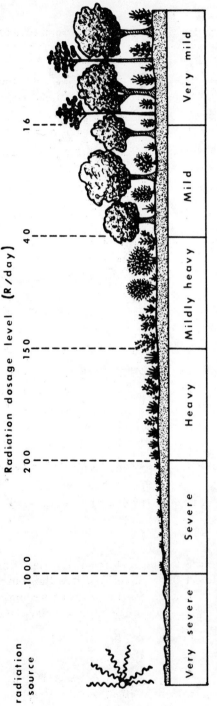

Figure 8.4. General responses of a terrestrial ecosystem to graded levels of stress (based upon the responses of a forest ecosystem to intense dosages of ionizing radiation). Symptoms of the graded stress include the following: *very mild stress*—reduction in growth rates of certain trees, *mild stress*—loss of some of the larger and more sensitive species of trees (especially the pines), *mildly heavy stress*—loss of all the trees, *heavy stress*—loss of all trees and shrubs, *severe stress*—loss of trees, shrubs, grasses, and herbs (only small ground lichens remain), *very severe stress*—loss of all vegetation and loss of topsoil through erosion. (This figure is based on data from Woodwell, 1970.)

TABLE 8.1
Some Generalized Biological Responses to Environmental Stress

1. *Responses at the level of the individual organism*
Metabolic interference. Supression or stimulation of respiration (related to degree of stress); accumulation of salts, lactic acid, and other metabolic wastes
Production of chemical "stress substances" (by invertebrates)
Modification of hormonal picture (evocation of the adreno-pituitary "general adaptation syndrome" of vertebrates)
Reproductive interference
Disorientation and death (in extreme stress)
2. *Responses at the level of the population*
Elimination of the most sensitive individuals
Modification of population size and age structure
Strong selection for genetically resistant forms
General decrease in genetic diversity within the population (with corresponding loss of adaptability)
Population extinction (in extreme stress)
3. *Responses at the level of the community-ecosystem*
Changes in the odds on competition, predation, parasitism, and disease
Changes in species composition through selective elimination of sensitive species and enhancement of resistant species
General reduction in standing crop and species diversity
Shift from closed to open nutrient cycles (resulting in partial or complete loss in nutrient reserves)
Shift from balance to imbalance; from stability to instability
Community collapse (in extreme cases)

toms of disturbance (Table 8.1) long before he is able to diagnose the specific agents responsible for the trouble. And it is the consensus of the community of practicing ecologists that the world ecosystems are now in serious trouble. The symptoms are widespread, and they are increasing daily.

Suggestions for Further Reading

CLARK, J. R. "Thermal Pollution and Aquatic Life." *Scientific American*, March 1969.
COOKE, L. M. et al. *Cleaning Our Environment, The Chemical Basis for Action.* Washington, D.C.: American Chemical Society, 1969.

CRONIN, L. E., and MANSUETI, A. J. "The Biology of the Estuary." In *A Symposium on the Biological Significance of Estuaries,* edited by P. A. Douglas and R. H. Stroud Washington, D.C.: Sport Fishing Institute, 1971.

EDWARDS, C. A. "Soil Pollutants and Soil Animals." *Scientific American,* April 1969.

HARTE, J., and SOCOLOW, R. H. *Patient Earth.* New York: Holt, Rinehart, and Winston, 1971.

KRENKEL, P. A., and PARKER, F. L. *Biological Aspects of Thermal Pollution.* Nashville: Vanderbilt University Press, 1969.

MRAK, E. M. et al. *Report of the Secretary's Commission on Pesticides and Their Relationship to Environmental Health.* Parts 1 and 2. Washington, D.C.: U.S. Department of Health, Education, and Welfare, December, 1969.

MURDOCH, W. W. et al. *Environment, Resources, Pollution & Society.* Stamford, Conn.: Sinauer Associates, 1971.

PEAKILL, D. B. "Pesticides and The Reproduction of Birds." *Scientific American,* April 1970.

POWERS, C. F., and ROBERTSON, A. "The Aging Great Lakes." *Scientific American,* November, 1966.

Report of the Study of Critical Environmental Problems (SCEP). *Man's Impact on the Global Environment.* Cambridge, Mass.: M.I.T. Press, 1970.

TRAIN, R. E.; CAHN, R.; and MACDONALD, G. J. *Environmental Quality, The First Annual Report of the Council on Environmental Quality.* Washington, D.C., 1970.

WOODWELL, G. M.; "Effects of Pollution on the Structure and Physiology of Ecosystems." *Science,* April 24, 1970.

WOODWELL, G. M.; CRAIG, P. P.; and JOHNSON, H. A. "DDT in the Biosphere: Where Does It Go?" *Science,* December 10, 1971.

YOUNG, G., and BLAIR, J. P. "Pollution, Threat to Man's Only Home." In "Our Ecological Crisis." *National Geographic,* December 1970.

9. the preservation of nature

The country in its pristine beauty, made up of heavy woodlands interspersed with prairie, was simply glorious. Birds of beautiful plumage were abundant, notably the oriole; and nature was musical with the fascinating call of the bobwhite, the plaintive note of the whippoorwill, the call of the mourning dove and the drumming of grouse. In the spring and fall the sky was darkened by flights of graceful passenger pigeons and immense flocks of ducks and geese, and occasionally we saw a flock of wild swans. On every side life was revelling amidst the utmost freedom. The lakes were pure, undefiled, and full of fish.
A. F. and B. Jackson

Early America

When Europeans landed on the North American continent, they encountered a land clothed in tall forests and magnificent prairies, of coastal marshes and cypress swamps, of clear lakes and fresh streams, of high mountains and extensive deserts. America was a land of great richness and biological diversity. The country was teeming with small game, wild fowl, deer, and endless herds of bison. A place of plenty, as well as beauty, America was for the pioneer a land of opportunity, and many an early explorer was moved to emotion when describing the abundance and green magnificence.

Prehistoric changes in the ecology of North America — But for all its beauty and ecological richness, the America of the explorers and settlers was not a virgin and undisturbed nature, as is often pictured. Asiatic man, who began arriving perhaps 25,000 to 50,000 years earlier, had already left major marks on the natural systems. Available evidence suggests that the earliest human immigrants consisted of wandering bands of food gatherers who subsisted upon vegetable products, clams, and small game. In the absence of evidence to the contrary, we assume that their influence was small, local, and temporary so that the natural systems healed the wounds and obliterated most of the records of the wandering tribes. We do know that the paleoindian lived in North America for thousands of years while the continent was still inhabited by a variety of giant mammals, the North American *megafauna*. Among the large herbivores were the wooly rhinoceros, wooly mammoth, Columbian elephant, giant ground sloth, American camels, giant bison, giant beaver, and several groups of large grazing mammals which have no close living relatives. The great predators included such forms as a saber-toothed cat which attacked from ambush, a large plains jaguar adapted for running down its prey, a plains bear, and the great dire wolf (Figure 9.1).

About 13,000 years ago there appeared on the American scene a group of paleohunters, highly skilled in the manufacture of flint-tipped weapons and culturally distinct from the early food gatherers. Within what seems, at this distance, to have been a few hundred years, these hunters spread widely throughout the habitable portions of North America, and we have ample documentation of the fact that these hunters successfully pursued the larger game. We also know that within about a thousand years of the first appearance of these hunters, approximately 70 percent of the large mammal species of North America had vanished from the earth. The megafauna, which had survived repeated climatic changes associated with advance and retreat of the continental glaciers, disappeared shortly after the hunters arrived. The period of the megafaunal extinction, from 13,000 to 12,000 years ago, was a time when most of the northern part of the continent was covered with glacial ice. It was a period of cold, wet weather, when our midwestern states were much like the steppes of Russia; a period of hardship, when many species of plants and animals were restricted to southern and coastal refuges where the climate was tolerable and food was ample.

Figure 9.1. Shadows of the past—a sampling of the Pleistocene megafauna of North America whose extinction was undoubtedly due, in part at least, to the activities of the paleohunters. Listed in order from left to right these include the wooly mammoth, American mastodon, large-horn bison, wooly rhinoceros, American camel, American plains cat, great North American short-faced bear, stag moose, saber-toothed cat, giant beaver, giant ground sloth, and dire wolf. Many more of the smaller species of plants and animals are known to have disappeared from North America as a result of past human activities, but the present rate of species extinction is without known parallel in the world's history. (This figure is based upon data from many sources, especially Martin, 1967, and Guthrie, 1972.)

It seems reasonable to conclude that despite the stresses of cold weather, restricted habitat, and reduced food supply, the large mammalian fauna might have again made a comeback if it had not simultaneously been confronted with the additional pressure of efficient super-predators which hunted in packs and killed from a distance with fire and sharp missiles. Man certainly had a major hand in the mass extinctions. With the larger fauna out of the way, the smaller species must have expanded to fill the recently vacated ecological gaps. Surely the smaller American bison, which survived to become the single major herbivore of the prairies, must have increased and occupied the ecological positions of its former competitor species, but what other adjustments took place we can only guess.

The paleohunter and his descendants were quite familiar with the use of fire, and it is reasonably clear that many of the fire-tolerant communities (i.e., some prairies, grasslands, and pine forests) encountered by the early Europeans were growing in areas which from climatic considerations should have been covered with hardwood forest climax. Furthermore, analysis of soil strata and pollen profiles from lake and bog sediments points to the fact that the hardwood forest was actually reached followed by a reversal to subclimax.

Even today many forest and prairie fires result from natural causes, but again the hand of man is evident. Fires often escape the careless camper, and the Indians were not notoriously careful. We know that they often set fires to drive game to convenient kill sites, and it is probable that they knew enough to utilize fire to maintain open grazing conditions. There is also the suggestion that fires were deliberately set to eliminate obnoxious neighbors downwind. Regardless of motivation or intent, the Indian's use of fire profoundly affected the ecology of the land. These few examples are sufficient to document the fact that when the first European stepped onto American soil, he encountered a set of ecosystems already modified and rather extensively managed. To this moment no one knows exactly what a "natural area" in North America should look like.

Historic changes in the ecology of North America — Civilized man develops high population densities. He utilizes the resources of his environment more fully than does primitive man, and he depletes and pollutes at a greater rate. With guns, axes, cows, and plows the settlers proceeded to drive out the Indians, remove the forest, burn the prairie, and plow the soil. In a westward march that reached the Pacific in the space of a few hundred years, he has eliminated all but a few remnants of the plant and animal communities which he forcibly inherited from the Indians. These developments, which proceeded slowly at first, began to pick up speed after the new nation was born. Industrialization hastened the process, and advanced technology has so buffered the masses of Americans that even the memory of the nature of the native woodlands and prairies has largely faded. Americans have been great writers, however, and sufficient written records have been left to sketch out the outlines of what has happened and what has been lost. Events which unfolded slowly elsewhere in the United States took place almost overnight on the West Coast following discovery of gold in California, and every American should make it a point to read Dasmann's dramatic and thoroughly documented account of *The Destruction of California*. This pattern of destruction has now doubled back on itself, and we are faced with the dismal prospect of the "californication" of the rest of the United States. This is the future which won't work.

Our focus here is not on the destruction of soil, air, and water; or the depletion of mineral resources; the massive urbanization syndrome; or even the marshalling of all aquatic resources into bizarre recirculating septic tanks. Rather, our attention and concern is directed toward a silent problem, but one which many ecologists perceive to be of even greater long-range import. This is the reckless abuse of the living resources of nature, begun by the aboriginal inhabitants and intensified by civilized man. Although we do not have a complete inventory of what was here at first, the plant and animal species, the communities and ecosystems, we do have some idea of what is left and of the processes still at work which are constantly whittling at the remaining splinters of nature. These processes are examined briefly below because they must be recognized and understood if they are to be widely appreciated and rectified.

The Forces of Destruction

Habitat elimination — One of the chief urges of civilized man is to convert "all that wasteland" into something "useful." Forest and prairie, brushland and desert, mountain and valley must have utility — but first it must be "cleared." Space is needed for housing, industry, highways, agriculture, airports, recreation, and all the other legitimate and illegitimate uses of which an industrialized people are capable. What happens when the last space is cleared? Or long before that, what happens when the last maple forest or tall-grass prairie or oak savanna falls to the developer?

Up until the present time, no one has ever been paid even to take stock of, let alone preserve, the diversity of America's living resources. State and Federal agencies have traditionally tended to equate "conservation" with "recreation," rather than with "preservation." As a result, no farmer realizes that his "back 40" contains the last living remnant of a particular community type. The housing developer or regional planner cannot know that a particularly desirable area for housing is really a small living relic of a once-widespread ecosystem type. Nor can the Army Corps of Engineers be expected to know that the dam they plan to construct will eliminate much of the native fish population and with it the clams whose larval forms depend upon the fish for transportation. No one has really been looking, and in the absence of authoritative information and vocal defenders, the silent species and the systems of nature have taken a real beating. So long as the bulldozer philosophy goes unchallenged, America's natural heritage becomes progressively impoverished.

Habitat homogenization — When man chopped down the forest, he established a yard. When he moved to the prairie, he planted trees around the house. When he settled in the desert, he added grass, shrubs, and trees, and sprinkled every afternoon. What is a yard and a garden? Is it a forest or a prairie? When man built a highway through the forest, he bordered it with grassy shoulders. When he staked out farms in the prairie, he established fence rows which grew up in briars and brush. The native plants and animals, formerly distributed in orderly fashion, are now terribly confused. Hybrid habitats have recently witnessed some weird interspecies miscegenation. As one ecologist put it, species which formerly would not touch each other with a ten foot pole are now behaving scandalously! How is a wild iris or a simple toad to know nowadays what is ecologically proper? The old constraints are gone. Environmental cues are all mixed up, and a new kind of evolution is proceeding in the man-modified habitats. Forest species invade the prairie along the fence row. Prairie species invade the woods along the road right-of-way. And they all meet in the garden. The American system of canals, dikes, dams, and pools has also disrupted life in the waters. Under the new set of ecological rules, the hardy will survive, the weak will be eliminated, and diversity will be reduced. Man and his weeds will prevail, and from coast to coast it will all be about the same.

Introduction of alien species — Throughout history, wherever mankind has traveled, he has been accompanied by a retinue of "social" species. These make up a long list and include such forms as household pets, domestic farm animals, rats, mice, roaches, bedbugs, lice, fleas, and houseflies. Each species, including man himself, has, in turn, been accompanied by a set of parasites and disease organisms. Agricultural man has brought along crop plants, together with a catalog of weed species, insects, and plant diseases. Industrial man, transporting raw materials from areas of production to sites of manufacture and use, has introduced a host of plant and animal species to new areas. Aesthetic man has imported countless species of flowers and ornamental plants, aquarium fishes, and birds. Sporting man has sought to increase the "action" through introduction of exotic game fishes, birds, and mammals. Some of the introductions have been accidental, others purposeful. What has been the result?

On the positive side, we have improved agricultural production, created thriving industries, and greatly added to our material welfare and esthetic comfort. On the negative side, we have burdened ourselves with a plague of pests, parasites, and diseases which must be held in check through the environmental dissemination of hundreds of tons of harsh chemicals and the annual expenditure of millions of dollars. On economic grounds perhaps we are ahead. Such a balance sheet, like many others we are accustomed to seeing nowadays, takes no account whatever of the side effects upon the natural systems. These are tacitly assumed to have no direct value; hence they do not even enter into most cost-evaluation calculations. But can they really be ignored?

Even aside from the large but poorly documented world-wide traffic of accidental introductions, the deliberate transport of plants and animals has become a major industry. For example, in 1968 alone over 64 million fishes are known to have been imported into North America from all corners of the globe. Many of the imports escape, and a great many others are purposely released to make their own ways among the native species. Fortunately, most of the alien species fail to establish themselves, but enough survive to make a real difference. We know that at least twenty-five exotic fish species now breed in our waters, and these include such forms as the widespread and destructive carp, and the very aggressive walking catfish, which is rapidly spreading from the site of its recent introduction into the waters of Florida. At least fifty alien species of mollusks and nineteen species of exotic aquatic plants are now established here.

In addition to the introduction from foreign lands, there has been extensive transplantation of plants and animals from one part of the country to another. For many of our states about half the fish fauna is now made up of exotic species (Table 9.1). The aliens which successfully become established do so, by and large, at the expense of the native flora and fauna. Directly through predation, competition, and hybridization, or indirectly through parasites and habitat alteration, they have led to or hastened the extinction of many of our endogenous species. Some, such as the carp, walking catfish, water hyacinth, and alligator weed have modified the native ecosystems to the point of no return.

To take one example, the State of Florida has been referred to as a biological cesspool. Fifty-seven species of exotic vertebrates now make their homes in the waters and forests of this state, a figure which is actually exceeded by the number of alien invertebrate species. Only Hawaii outranks Florida in the number of successful introductions. New to the Floridean vertebrate fauna are fifteen species of mammals, twelve species of birds, seventeen species of reptiles, three species of amphibians, and ten species of fishes! Even if we somehow manage to preserve the Everglades, what have we got?

Another side of the matter deserves mention. We have so far been spared from many species of plants and animals which live in other parts of the world whose introduction could result in severe consequences for both man and nature. The mongoose has created real trouble wherever it has obtained a foothold. Several South American spiders of the "brown recluse" family are not only deadly, but they are exceedingly aggressive, attacking large animals, including humans, with impunity. A very aggressive African bee has recently become a real problem in South America, and it may soon find its way north. A tiny South American catfish, the *candiru,* is dreaded by the natives because of its tendency to penetrate the urogenital openings of men and women bathers, as well as other animals which enter the water. Their backward-projecting spines prevent easy removal, and surgery is generally necessary to stop the pain, inflammation, infection, and hemorrhaging. Several species of the deadly carnivorous piranha are still sold in tropical fish stores throughout the country, but so far they are not known to have become established in our lakes and streams. For detailed case histories of some of the more important animal introductions, the reader is referred to an excellent recent book by George Laycock, *The Alien Animals.* That writer concludes that, "Release of wildlife into territory foreign to it involves, not a calculated risk, but a risk too great to calculate." How can the risk be ignored by government and "cost-benefit" people alike? Only a little reflection is necessary to realize that the aggressive exotics, whether plant or animal, are really potentially dangerous "weeds," and that their introduction and dissemination is nothing more nor less than biological pollution. This form of pollution is unique, however, in that it is capable of spreading far and wide from the original site of release, all the while multiplying itself manyfold.

TABLE 9.1

State	Total number of species known from waters of the state	Native species (%)	Alien species (%)
Arizona	65	43	57
California	67	52	48
Colorado	87	62	38
Connecticut	53	55	45
Nevada	62	66	34
Utah	50	52	48

Composition of the freshwater fish fauna of selected states where accurate records are available. Note that less than half the fish species now inhabiting the waters of Arizona are native to the State. The rest have been derived from accidental or intentional introductions.

Species Extinction

Four primary pressures are now directed at the native American flora and fauna: habitat elimination, habitat homogenization, and struggle with alien species (discussed above), as well as environmental pollution (discussed in the previous chapter). Analysis of any particular case history may reveal that one or another of these factors is predominant; more often the restriction or demise of a species results from a combination of these factors acting together. But what has actually been lost, and what is in danger of being lost?

In 1966 the U.S. Department of the Interior published a document entitled, *Rare and Endangered Fish and Wildlife of the United States.* The tabulation includes only vertebrate animals, and no parallel document giving account of the plants or lower animals has yet appeared. Included in the volume is a list of vertebrate animals known to have become *extinct* in historic time, as well as accounts of those known to be *endangered* (prospects for survival are in immediate jeopardy), *rare* (small populations which could be threatened if the environment worsens), and *peripheral* (species found also outside the United States, but which are rare or endangered only in the U.S. portion of their ranges). Also included are species of *status undetermined* (suspect of being endangered, but too poorly known to tell for sure). This information is summarized in Table 9.2.

Forty-eight different kinds of vertebrates are known to have disappeared during the recent past, and this list is unquestionably too low be-

TABLE 9.2

Vertebrate group	Rare and endangered	Peripheral	Status undetermined	Totals
Mammals	33	8	5	46
Birds	50	60	51	161
Reptiles	4	2	8	14
Amphibians	5	0	8	13
Fishes	38	4	45	87
Totals	130	74	117	321

Vertebrate animals native to the United States which are known or suspected to be in danger of extinction (as of 1966). The category headings are explained in the text.

cause the early records are quite incomplete. Included in the known list are such forms as the Plains wolf, New England sea mink, Eastern cougar, Steller's sea cow, Eastern elk, Merriam elk, Badlands bighorn sheep, Labrador duck, Heath hen, Great auk, Passenger pigeon, Mauge's parakeet, Carolina parakeet, Louisiana parakeet, San Gorgonio trout, Harelip sucker, Leon Springs pupfish, and Ash Meadows killifish. These are gone forever. Among the rare and endangered types are a bat, squirrel, wolves, fox, bear, ferret, panther, seals, sea cow, pronghorn, three geese, three ducks, condor, kite, hawk, bald eagle, prairie chicken, bobwhite, whooping crane, woodpecker, warblers, sparrows, alligator, lizard, snake, salamander, toad, sturgeon, whitefish, five trout, minnows, pike, pupfish, and killifishes.

All told, 327 native vertebrates are gone or are likely to go soon if nothing is done — 46 mammals, 180 birds, 13 reptiles, 11 amphibians, and 77 fishes among the vertebrates alone. How much are they worth, and how many can we afford to lose? A bit further down the road are hundreds more waiting to pass through the endangered list to oblivion. And with the vertebrates go hundreds upon uncounted hundreds of lower animals and plants. Forward progress in human society is marked by reverse progress in nature.

As the individual species dwindle to a few populations and then disappear, the ecosystems of which they were a part must constantly readjust to the loss of individual components. If top predators are removed, populations of smaller predators expand. If intermediate predators are removed, the top predators collapse and the herbivores get out of hand. If the herbivores are destroyed, all the predators are in trouble. If the plants go, the animals disappear. In most natural ecosystems there is considerable redundancy, and elimination of one species seldom shows such dramatic results unless it happens to be a key species. But with nonselective poisons, pesticides, and herbicides, man has recently devised means of eliminating broad categories of animals and plants. In any event, when one portion of an ecosystem is in trouble, the rest of the ecosystem is unlikely to remain unaffected. Most of the trouble escapes the attention of the individual, company, or agency applying the pressure, especially since they are seldom looking.

Reversal of a Trend

About two decades ago the Conservation Department of the State of Wisconsin developed plans for the establishment of a pine forest on an old field in southeastern Wisconsin. There was apparently no way the Department could know that this particular field was visited regularly by University botanists and their field classes and that the tract was considered to be the finest remnant of undisturbed prairie left in the southeastern part of the state. When word finally reached the University, the Conservation Department was contacted, and the afforestation plan was dropped. The episode might have ended there, but to men of vision in the Conservation Department, Department of Public Instruction, State University, and Milwaukee Public Museum, a case had been made. An advisory body was needed to insure that lands of especial value were not lost. Through the cooperative action of these agencies and the State Legislature, there was created by statute a State board to "formulate policies for the preservation, selection, acquisition, and management of areas necessary for scientific research, the teaching of conservation and natural history, and for the preservation of rare or valuable plant and animal species and communities." (Wisconsin statute 23.27)

Through the research of Dr. John T. Curtis and other scientists, the vegetational communities of Wisconsin were quite well known (more so probably than in any other state), and the State Board for the Preservation of Scientific Areas decided that one of its chief goals was to locate and achieve permanent preservation of representative examples of each community type appearing in Dr. Curtis' vegetational classification scheme (Table 9.3). Later the state was divided into four sections, and efforts were made to achieve preservation of every community type occurring within each quadrant. Whereas, the board was also interested in preserving the native animals, it was considered that the best way of accomplishing this would be to set aside and maintain a diverse series of plant communities.

At the present writing, the Wisconsin Scientific Area System now approaches 100 carefully selected representative sites already set aside. With traditionally strong citizen support and nonpartisan legislative backing, the system will continue to grow until representation is complete. Future residents will know what a prairie looks like, and in fact, they may examine a dozen different types of prairie if they wish. More important, the scientists will be able to study processes of soil formation, plant succession on permanent quadrats, growth and yield of native vegetation, long-term growth cycles, composition and fluctuation in insect populations, microclimates associated with different community types, the flow of nutrients and energy. The "field laboratories" are being set aside for investigation of how ecosystems function, and in this regard they provide natural baselines against which modified environments may be measured.

Aldo Leopold, one of the great Wisconsin ecologists, once wrote, "One cannot study the physiology of Montana to the Amazon: each biotic province needs its own wilderness for comparative studies of used and unused land. It is of course too late to salvage more than a lop-sided system of wilderness remnants, and most of these are far too small to retain their normality. All wilderness areas, no matter how small or imperfect, have a large value to land science. The important thing is to realize that recreation is not their only or even their principal, utility."

TABLE 9.3

Distinguishing Features			Communities	Representative Species
Mature Trees Present	Savannas (Scattered trees)		*Hardwoods dominant*	
			1. Oak Barren	Black oak, Hills oak
			2. Oak Opening	White oak, Bur oak
			Conifers dominant	
			3. Pine Barren	Jack pine
			4. Cedar Glade	Red cedar
	Forests		*Hardwoods only*	
			5. Southern Dry Forest	Black oak, White oak
			6. Southern Dry-mesic Forest	Red oak, Elm
			7. Southern Mesic Forest	Maple, Basswood
			8. Southern Wet-mesic Forest	Soft maple, Ash, Elm
			9. Southern Wet Forest	Willow, Cottonwood
			Mixed Conifers and Hardwoods	
			10. Northern Dry Forest	Jack pine, Aspen
			11. Northern Dry-mesic Forest	Pine, Red oak, Maple
			12. Northern Mesic Forest	Maple, Hemlock, Yellow birch
			13. Northern Wet-mesic Forest	White cedar, Ash
			Conifers only	
			14. Northern Wet Forest	Black spruce, Tamarack
			15. Boreal Forest	Balsam fir, Spruce
Mature Trees Absent	Terrestrial		*Shrubs dominant*	
			16. Shrub-Carr	Willow, Dogwood
			17. Alder Thicket	Speckled alder
			18. Open bog	Sphagnum, Leatherleaf
			Herbs dominant	
			Closed Communities	
			19. Northern Sedge Meadow	Sedges, Blue joint
			20. Southern Sedge Meadow	Sedges, Cord grass
			21. Fen	Blue joint, Mana grass
			22. Dry Prairie	Little Bluestem, Gramma grass
			23. Dry-mesic Prairie	Bluestem, Little Bluestem
			24. Mesic Prairie	Bluestem, Needlegrass
			25. Wet-mesic Prairie	Bluestem, Blue joint
			26. Wet Prairie	Blue joint, Cord grass
			27. Bracken Grassland	Bracken, Poverty grass
			Open Communities	
			28. Open Cliff Community	Campion, Cliff-brake
			29. Shaded Cliff Community	Polypody, Fragile fern
			30. Sand Barren	Junegrass, Little Bluestem
			31. Beach Community	Sea-rocket, Saltwort
			32. Lake Dune Community	Beachgress, Beach pea
	Aquatic		33. Emergent Aquatics	Cat-tail, Bur-reed
			34. Submerged Aquatics	Pondweed, Eelgrass

Classification of plant community types occurring in the State of Wisconsin. (Modified after Curtis, 1959.)

The Wisconsin system is a model of enlightened land use, but it does not stand alone. About half the states have by now recognized the problem and have begun to do something about it, with varying degrees of success. These progressive states, by and large, lie in the upper Midwest, eastward to New England and southward through the mid-Atlantic states. The reader might well ask what is being done in his own state.

It would be unfair to conclude this chapter without reference to certain other efforts to establish natural area systems. In the private sector, The Nature Conservancy, Sierra Club, and Audubon Society have been especially effective and deserve greatly increased public support. The Federal Government has begun to take an active interest in locating important sites within the federal land holdings with the intent of establishing a system of Research Natural Areas broadly representative of the forest and grassland types listed in the federal classification system. Under the auspices of the International Biological Programme, the U.S. Subcommittee for the Conservation of Ecosystems has been attempting for several years to develop a better system for classification of aquatic and terrestrial community types and to locate representative areas throughout the United States which are still in reasonably natural condition and which should be preserved if at all possible. Although these endeavors are proceeding independently, the personnel involved are in general communication with one another, united in a common resolve to save something of primitive America for tomorrow. Poorly funded and often only tolerated by administrations, a handful of scientists and lay citizens are intensively involved in a salvage operation still generally misunderstood and officially viewed as uneconomic. The extinction of species and communities has been taking place since life first appeared on earth, but a large body of distinguished environmental scientists now holds the view that never before in the earth's history has the rate of extinction reached the intensity and widespread proportions now in effect. The efforts of a few to reverse this trend may prove to be too little and too late, but at present this is the only hope for those native species and communities now on the brink of oblivion.

Suggestions for Further Reading

Bureau of sport Fisheries and Wildlife. *Rare and Endangered Fish and Wildlife of the United States.* Washington, D.C., U.S. Department of the Interior. Resource Publication 34, 1966.

Cruikshank, H. G. *John and William Bartram's America.* New York: Natural History Library, Doubleday & Co., 1961.

Dasman, R. F. *Environmental Conservation.* New York: John Wiley & Sons, 1968.

————. *The Destruction of California.* New York: Collier Books, 1969.

ELTON, C. S. *The Ecology of Invasions by Animals and Plants.* London: Methuen, 1958.

FISHER, J.; SIMON, N.; and VINCENT, J. *Wildlife in Danger.* New York: Viking Press, 1969.

GUTHRIE, R. D., "A Look at Alaska's Tundra, Its Amazing Past." *National Geographic,* March 1972.

HARDIN, G. *Nature and Man's Fate.* New York: New American Library, 1959.

LACHNER, E. A.; ROBINS, C. R.; and COURTENAY, W. R., Jr. "Exotic Fishes and Other Aquatic Organisms Introduced into North America." *Smithsonian Contributions to Zoology,* no. 59. Washington, D.C.: Smithsonian Institution Press, 1970.

LAYCOCK, G. *The Alien Animals.* Garden City, N.Y.: Natural History Press, 1966.

LEOPOLD, A. *A Sand County Almanac.* New York: Oxford University Press, 1949.

MARTIN, P. S. "Pleistocene Overkill." *Natural History,* December 1967.

MARTIN, P. S., and WRIGHT, H. E., eds. *Pleistocene Extinctions: Search for a Cause.* New Haven, Conn.: Yale University Press, 1967.

McVAY, S. "The Last of the Great Whales." *Scientific American,* August 1966.

10. tomorrow

. . . As history moves on, our time will be known as the age in which man learned to admit that he is part of the balance of nature—the age in which man joined his perspective on technology with a perspective on his environment . . .

Stewart L. Udall

In the last three chapters we have examined in some detail the three primary problems facing human society: unrestricted growth in human numbers, reduction in environmental quality through the introduction of a variety of agents which induce stress on biological systems, and the wanton destruction of our native ecosystems with accompanying impoverishment of the native flora and fauna. To facilitate immediate recall, we refer to these problems as the three "P's": population, pollution, and preservation. Together, these three factors add up to a single common multiplier which is the *environmental impact of the world population.* A clear understanding of this concept is essential to place all other problems in perspective and to lay the groundwork for rational decisions concerning future policy toward ourselves, our nation, and our one world.

Living Standards and Environmental Impact

Although severe local problems exist, the world is not yet overcrowded, as such. A great many more people could be supported by this planet if we were willing to settle for subsistence living standards and if we were knowledgeable and wise enough to marshall the world's environmental resources for optimum distribution and use. However, all of our accumulated experience points to the fact that mankind will struggle to better his lot. From our present perspective it seems axiomatic that, given the opportunity, man will endeavor to increase his own living standards, especially if he perceives that his own standards are below those of his neighbors. But high population and high living standards are, in the long run, incompatible.

Figure 10.1 explores the relationships between world population level and environmental impact, given the assumption of rising average standards of living. If the population is permitted to increase, then the environmental impact rises at a very rapid rate (which may be described by the factor, $e^{(i+r)t}$, as discussed in Chapter 7). Assuming a stable world population, the environmental impact still increases in response to the rise in living standards. This, in fact, is the fallacy of the theory of "zero population growth," since the environment is still deteriorating with a stable population. (In fact, even if both population and living conditions are held constant, there would still be some deterioration because recycling is never 100 percent efficient. Therefore, it will take increasing increments of effort just to "stay even.") On the other hand, suppose it is decided that environmental impact must remain stable at all costs (as eventually it must). Then, if the living standards are to increase, the population must be forced into a decline.

We now encounter one of the ultimate problems facing civilization. Environmental deterioration cannot be allowed to increase indefinitely. Within the context of a tolerable environmental impact, what combination of world population level and average living standard shall we decide upon? A related, but perhaps more basic question, concerns the decision as to where to set the environmental impact level. As shown in Figure 10.2, four possible courses of action are open to us.

A. If the environmental impact goal is set too low, then we will be forced to retreat to low civilization or to some pastoral way of life where the population is too sparse and life is too simple to provide the goods and services required by a complex society. Indeed, there are many advocates of this alternative, but it seems highly unlikely that society, as a whole, having glimpsed the fruits of technology, will lightly abandon their harvest. The simple life must be held open as a position of possible retreat in case of necessity, but it cannot be embraced as the ultimate goal if a more desirable alternative is still available.

B. At a somewhat higher environmental impact level, complex civilization is possible which is based upon a fairly high population coupled with moderately high living standards. In order to last, the world resources would have to be carefully programmed, recycling would have to be fairly efficient, and the entire program would have to be understood and supported by society, at large. This goal, which I have called the *optimum*, is our window to the future. Through this opening, population could presumably survive in reasonable comfort indefinitely.

C. Above the optimum is the zone of environmental stress in which the greatly simplified environment could continue to support the human population, at least for awhile. For very high population levels the living standards must be low, and the world would become "ghettoized" everywhere. For low populations we might all live like kings, but for

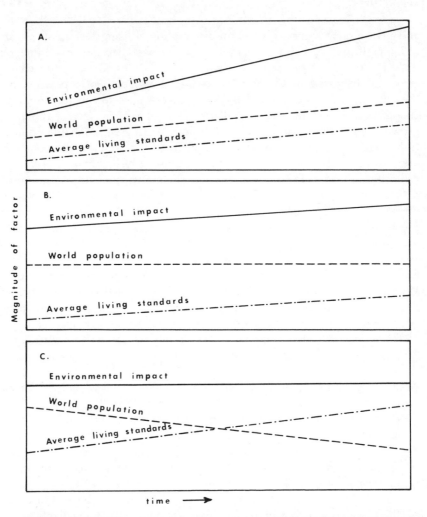

Figure 10.1. Relationships between world population and environmental impact, assuming a continued rise in average living standards. A. If the world population continues to increase, very rapid environmental deterioration is inevitable. B. If the world population remains stable, the environment deteriorates only in direct response to living-standard increase. C. If the environmental impact is held constant (as eventually it must be), increase in average living standards automatically dictates a decrease in human population size. These conclusions are based on the premise that average living standards and environmental impact are necessarily and directly related. The author knows of no information that can successfully refute this argument. Technological advances may remove some of the impact from high human visibility, but the overall environmental effect remains. Additionally, each advance spawns new consumer demands which, in the present society, must be met by elected officials and profit-motivated industry. What alternatives are available?

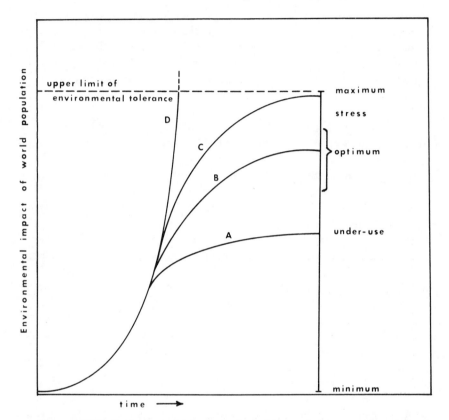

Figure 10.2. Environmental impact of world population as a function of time. Four possible destinies are presented. A. The environmental impact is low, and resources are wasted or at least not utilized to capacity. B. The impact stabilizes within the optimum zone. C. The impact settles in the possibly tolerable but highly undesirable upper zone of environmental stress. D. The environmental impact exceeds tolerable levels, quickly exhausting the resources and destroying the life-support system. Unfortunately, science is not yet capable of defining the precise upper limits of environmental tolerance, and present information strongly suggests that we are following path D.

how long? World resources would be perilously impoverished, and long-range survival would depend upon most careful attention to resource distribution, use, and reuse. The margin for environmental mistakes would be quite thin.

D. Finally, we must assume that there is somewhere a maximum level beyond which continued environmental abuse would lead inexorably to exhaustion of resources and destruction of the life-support system. Even short-term flirtation with this zone must inevitably be followed by population crash and dramatic reduction of living standards everywhere.

The above analysis is based upon an analogy. In the first chapter (especially in Figure 1.4), it was pointed out that with respect to environmental factors, an organism exhibits a range of tolerance, upper and lower zones of stress, and an optimum range. I now contend that when one organism, such as man, becomes the dominant factor, modifying all the living systems of the planet, then the environment itself (through its living systems) responds as though it were the organism and man were the environment. It is often dangerous to carry analogies too far, but within the present context and to the extent the analogy has been drawn, the comparison appears valid. In our relationships with the environment, we must at least think in terms of optimum range, upper zone of stress, and maximum limit of tolerance of the environment itself.

At the present time we still have many choices left open to us. But the longer we defer, the more difficult will be the decisions, the more costly the solutions, and the fewer will be the available options. On a regional basis, many of the world's nations are already in the upper zone of stress from population alone. Attempting to increase their living standards without reducing their populations is sheer folly. We ourselves are entering the stress zone, not so much from population, but from high living standards. Continuing to increase our standards of living without reducing the population is environmental irresponsibility of the worst kind, since we at least are in a position to make the choice. Their problem is gonadal, ours cerebral. Their fate is famine, ours gluttony. World and national leaders must become acutely aware of these problems and of the available solutions, and they must not fail to act soon. The interface of science and society must occupy the center of the political arena, and the public itself must understand and support the environmental decisions ahead.

Steps in the Right Direction

We have been examining the roots of world environmental problems on a grand scale, but the problems cannot be solved on such a basis. They must be broken down to more specific subproblems and scaled on a more local level before they can be attacked realistically. In the present section, brief attention will be given to a series of the more important specific problems, and pathways for solution will be examined.

Controlling world population — As pointed out in Chapter 7, population growth in the United States has slowed down to where it is now only slightly greater than zero. Whether this represents a real trend or simply a short-term postponement of families is not clear, but surely, in this country and in most of the other developed nations, we could achieve zero growth or even population decline rather quickly and painlessly if this became absolutely necessary. What about the rest of the world, the "have nots" who aspire to our living standards but who seem destined to sink further behind? No one at present has any realistic inkling as to how this problem can be resolved. Although a variety of birth-control methods is now available, how can they realistically be applied to masses of semi-starved illiterates? Vasectomy (cutting of the spermatic cords in males) is certainly one of the easiest, cheapest, and most effective ways of preventing conception and one free of many primitive religious taboos, and this may yet prove to be the ultimate answer. But to carry out such a major program of human sterilization calls for organization, financial support, and public acceptance on a scale unheard of in these nations in the past. Perhaps if our foreign aid took the form of or was tied to some sterilization incentive, the program might work. A great deal of scientific investigation is currently being carried out in the area of reproduction control, and major breakthroughs are anxiously awaited. The populations will, of course, eventually be controlled, if not by sterilization then by starvation or by population-related wars, such as the recent India-Pakistan hostility. This population problem must stand as one of the major unsolved world problems of our time.

Reduction of pollution — It may be said of civilization that waste is our most important product. Mountains of raw materials are processed, utilized, and discarded in mountains of solid wastes. These trashpiles are becoming valuable sources of raw materials for recycling, however, and the day is not far off when solid wastes will be considered a valuable resource. A larger problem arises from the gaseous and finely particulate material that enters the atmosphere from chimneys and exhausts and the chemicals which enter our streams. Once they become diluted and dispersed, their recovery is impossible. Unfortunately, there is a vast gap between the level necessary for economic retrieval and what is still toxic. To be economically recoverable most major resources must be present at least in parts per hundred or parts per thousand. But many substances are toxic in a few parts per million, and some are deadly when dilute as one part per hundred million (less than a spoonful in a swimmingpool). The interesting thing about pollution is that as we poison nature we also poison ourselves, and we will certainly put a stop to that. Unfortunately, many of the biocides do not seem to affect us directly, either because we are less sensitive than many other creatures or because the poisons pass primarily through soil and water, seldom coming back to us except as an allergy or occasionally at the dinner table. Will we be wise enough to stop the pollution which does not seem to create imminent human health hazards? For the most part we will. The great majority of environmental pollutants can be trapped and recovered at the source, before they enter the atmosphere and surface waters. For a little extra financial burden we can enjoy a healthier environment, and it is becoming clear that the voters will demand it.

A major problem still exists in relation to agricultural chemicals (fertilizers, insecticides, and herbicides). Improved agricultural practices, an enlarged portfolio of less-damaging and less-persistent agrochemicals, coupled with a more enlightened approach should help greatly in this area. In general, farmers and ranchers should be encouraged to employ chemicals specific to the targets rather than broad-spectrum biocides (the "rifle" rather than the "shotgun" approach). The use of insect hormones, specific parasites and predators (biological control), and the release of sterile males of a noxious species, all have considerable promise. In any event, efforts should be made to prevent damaging or persistent chemicals from entering the waterways and the atmosphere. The enormous use of agrochemicals by the underdeveloped nations to stave off disease and starvation presents a serious unsolved problem which will be with us for some time, and the only answer here is the call for extensive research aimed at solving the problems with less environmental damage. The advent of less-persistent pesticides is promising in this regard.

The establishment of ecological preserves — Somehow it runs counter to our traditional value systems that public funds should be spent on the establishment of areas from which the public would be excluded. This is so only because we are used to focusing upon proximate rather than ultimate goals. We must, however, begin thinking of nature as our bank accounts. The checking account is available for day-to-day use, but in the background is the savings account which can bail us out when we overdraw the checking account. A world-wide system of natural areas, representative of the world's remaining ecological diversity, must be established as a back-up account against unwise use of the remaining biological resources. We are not yet wise enough to understand the workings of nature, and decent sites for sophisticated analytic study of nature are becoming alarmingly scarce. Nor are we wise enough to know all the ways in which nature may serve us, the medicines and industrial products which plants and animals may yield, the genetic raw materials for crop and livestock improvement. What will be needed by future generations can only be guessed, and it behooves us to provide them with the tools to correct our own unwitting errors. The savings account also becomes the trust fund.

So far no major political party has been willing to include nature preservation in its platform or in its operating policy, once in office. Yet a carefully selected system of nature preserves is surely an ecological necessity. If anything may be considered an "ecological imperative," this certainly is. Much preservation work can be accomplished at the local as well as the national levels, and far-sighted ecologically minded citizens would do well to educate office seekers, legislators, and administrators of this important, overlooked environmental task.

The development of protective environmental legislation — Our legal system provides batteries of laws for safeguarding persons and private property, and it has established rules which must be followed in transacting business and amassing personal and corporate wealth. However, by and large, those areas which we all hold and use in common and which we have come to accept as free, are not so protected. The air, inland waters, open seas, and world ecosystems are common properties which we use and abuse with no payment and little fear of legal restraint or retaliation.

In pioneer days there was little need to worry about the "commons," but when the population density is high, the frontier philosophy just will not work. We share the environment too closely to be immune to the effects of others. In basic ecology we encounter the same phenomenon under the category of "indirect effects." A coyote which eats a prairie dog exerts a direct effect, but an oak tree which shades the ground indirectly affects the grass and ground-dwelling animals through environmental modification. In society, as in nature, the indirect effects may be quite as important as the direct effects, but considerable ground must yet be broken in this underdeveloped area of environmental law.

A related matter in need of legal attention concerns the rights of the public, as a whole, to land held in private ownership. Should an individual property owner have the right to degrade land for temporary profit, thereby depriving all future owners of the inherent value of the same land? Where do private rights end and public sovereignty begin? The economy of any nation is based ultimately upon the land and what it can produce, but in the absence of explicit protective legislation, the individual owner may generally assume that all the rights are vested in himself.

A good beginning is found in Article IX, Section 3 of the Constitution of the State of Wisconsin which reads as follows:

> Ultimate property in lands: escheats. Section 3. The people of the state, in their right of sovereignty, are declared to possess the ultimate property, in and to all lands within the jurisdiction of the state; and all lands the title to which shall fail from a defect of heirs shall revert or escheat to the people.

The people are clearly recognized as the ultimate owners of the land. But does this statement go far enough, and do other states similarly recognize public rights to private property?

Under the U. S. Constitution there are only three ways of controlling land for public benefit: 1) the *approval system* — in which an owner must seek a permit to modify his property in certain ways, 2) *police power* — whereby property use may be restricted through legal zoning ordinances, and 3) *outright purchase* — with or without the use of condemnation proceedings. But on what grounds may public interest suits be brought for private land degradation and abuse? Where is the legal foundation?

To establish in no uncertain terms the right of the public to clean air, clean inland waters, and clean seas and to protect the land from abuse by private owners, nothing less than a constitutional amendment will do. We do not yet have an "Environmental Bill of Rights," nor will we without public insistence. Meanwhile, our national heritage disappears before our eyes.

National and international land-and-water-use plans — With resources at a premium, with pollution already exceeding tolerable levels in many areas, we still operate largely by crisis rather than by design. We know that certain land and water uses are compatible with one another, whereas other uses are totally incompatible. A given estuary may well support industry, shipping, and heavy urbanization, but it cannot at the same time continue to provide for commercial fishing, recreation, and species preservation. Why is it that we cannot decide on a regional basis to use one estuary on a coastline for heavy pressures and set aside another for light use? Does every stream have to be dammed, every bay dredged, every marsh filled, every estuary polluted?

Part of the problem resides in failure of government to take cognizance of the multiple pressures. But the heart of the difficulty seems to lie in the jurisdictional hierarchy involved. States scream about "states rights" and tell the federal government to keep out. Counties tell the states to keep out, municipalities tell the counties to lay off, and individual property owners (including the major corporations which hold vast acreages of land) protect their land interests with a vengeance. This jurisdictional game has all but walled citizens off from the coastlines, and on the Great Lakes it is hard for a citizen even to see the lakes unless he happens to own a piece of shoreline property.

Taking the matter one step further, the United States could not clean up the Gulf of Mexico through unilateral action, nor could Denmark alone do much about pollution in the North Sea. Some problems must be faced by those at the top of a given hierarchy, and the need for rational planning of large scope increases with every passing day. But plans serve no useful purpose if they are not backed up by funds for implementation and legal authority for penalizing noncompliance. The day of rational, large-scale environmental design must soon arrive, for the longer it is delayed, the more formidable will be the problems, and the fewer will be our options.

Balancing ecology and economy — Economic gain and establishment of creature comfort have been among the chief driving forces of the technological civilization, and we have been remarkably successful in fulfilling these desires. A broader perspective on the future has revealed that our goals, if not misdirected, are at least incomplete. If our children and theirs are to enjoy the fruits of our labor, if we care at all about what is ahead, we must temper our material apetites for the long haul. The environment can tolerate only so much stress, and we must redirect science and technology to provide specific knowledge about tolerance levels of the life-support systems of this planet. That is the heart of the ecology message, and it cannot long be ignored. Once we know where the breaking point of nature is, then we can proceed to make decisions as to where we wish to stop short. It may be that there is no one specific point of breakage, just a general breakdown everywhere, with the final life system being a few kinds of green plants, mankind, and a few kinds of bacteria to provide the simplest recycling system possible. Beyond that, perhaps technology can replace the plants and bacteria, leaving us alone with our machines. Assuming it is feasible, is this what we want? Or should we begin now to work out a balance somewhere short of the ultimate?

The Search for the Truth

The need for technical knowledge — Goethe once said, "There is nothing more frightening than ignorance in action," and were he living today, he might well have directed this statement to our response to the environmental crisis. We have recently witnessed scientists, representatives of industry, and government officials jumping in all directions in frank admission of ignorance on vital environmental matters. We have seen charge and emotional countercharge. But in the aftermath of the emotional crisis, can we really assess the extent of our environmental ignorance? Observing ecosystems under stress, we are in some cases able to associate specific symptoms with particular causes, but in a great many instances, the stress agents are unrevealed by the symptoms. Often we do not know the causes, nor are we likely to find out without a massive effort to do so. A doctor must understand the healthy body before he can prescribe for a sick one. And so it is with ecosystems.

Of the hundreds of thousands of different chemical compounds manufactured and released into the environment by man, it is certain that we have adequate knowledge of the biogeochemical adventures of but a few. Nor do our technical journals yet tell us much about the specific effects of many of these on biological systems, let alone their effects when acting in combination. What happens when an individual shrimp contains DDT, DDD, DDE, lindane, aldrin, dieldrin, heptachlor, methoxychlor, and other chlorinated hydrocarbons for a total body concentration in excess of 55 ppm, all at the same time (as some of the shrimp are now showing)? What happens to humans who have such body loads? We cannot expect to make wise decisions about use practices without specialized knowledge of a very technical nature. The search for such knowledge begins in the laboratory, and fortunately this search is now well under way.

Multidisciplinary approaches — There is also a need for knowledge at another level. The problems with which we are now faced, are by and large multifaceted. Total answers to such problems do not arise from any single set of specialists, and they cannot be resolved by any single segment of society. Rather, they call for concerted action of multidisciplinary teams of specialists and generalists who together may discern the various alternatives facing society so that options are laid out and consequences of specific courses of action are clearly available for wise decision making. In recognition of this need, many groups and institutions, from the United Nations on down, are now engaged in a series of complex meetings, conferences, and workshops, each aimed at providing perspective on multifaceted problems of our times. An example of the informational input into one such recent conference dealing with complex coastal-zone problems is given in Table 10.1. This type of approach is clearly the forerunner of things to come. The communication gap between disciplines must be bridged.

Public education and the truth — In his numerous writings, Thomas Jefferson revealed an unshakable faith in the ability of ordinary citizens to reach correct decisions concerning matters of their own government, and history has not yet proven him wrong. But in the recent past, a great many decisions which affect all our lives have been made behind closed doors, with the public learning of them after it is too late to investigate the real facts and too late to mount effective opposition. Suddenly aware that we are losing our environment by default, the public is now demanding open hearings on matters which affect our lives. Ordinary people are participating in the decision making as never before in recent times.

As the most educated, alert, and vocal people in history, we, as citizens, are attempting to cope with exceedingly complex environmental problems. But spunk alone is not sufficient to prepare citizens to police their own environments. More than ever before there exists the need for direct communication between scientist and citizen; for sophisticated public defenders, independent of government; for environmental action groups to ferret out the facts revealing what is behind the scenes and below the surface. Here is a job for everyone. In a recent address to the American Chemical Society, Mr. William D. Ruckleshaus, Administrator for the Environmental Protection Agency, expressed the need for open communication with the public quite forcefully and clearly.

> . . . First, I am convinced that if a decision regarding the use
> of a particular chemical is to have credibility with the public,

TABLE 10.1

I. Social, Economic and Legal Problems

Working Group 1   *Demography and Land Use:*
population density, growth and distribution patterns
in the coastal zone

Working Group 2   *Municipal, Industrial and Recreational Use:*
growth, diversification, and intensification of human
utilization of the coastal zone

Working Group 3   *Legislative and Legal Aspects:*
existing laws and desirable changes in legal restrictions
relating to the coastal zone, and methods of achieving
the necessary legislation

II. Physical and Chemical Problems

Working Group 4   *Hydrographic and Meteorological Factors:*
climatic effects on land and sea, circulation and mixing in coastal waters

Working Group 5   *Exploitation of Nonrenewable Resources:*
presently exploited and potential mineral resources of
the coastal zone, methods of exploitation and transport, and potential for immediate environmental
damage

Working Group 6   *Pollutants in the Coastal Zone:*
classes of pollutants, sites of injection, transport,
ultimate fates

III. Biological and Ecological Problems

Working Group 7   *Fisheries Resources:*
commercially important species, life histories, present
and potential harvest, possibilities of increase through
environmental manipulation and cultivation

Working Group 8   *Ecological Effects of Man's Activities on the Coastal
Zone:*
effects of habitat modification, harvest pressure, and
effects of pollution on coastal species and ecosystems

Working Group 9   *Habitats and Conservation:*
existing and needed preserves, species and ecosystem
methods of achieving preservation and system stability
in the face of mounting environmental pressure

IV. Coastal Zone Management in the Future

Working Group 10   *Regional Planning and Systems Analysis:*
components and interrelationships for the coastal
zone master plan of the future

Types of informational input into a recent multidisciplinary conference
dealing with critical problems of the coastal zone. The ultimate aim of
such conferences is to reduce the environmental impact of continued and
expanding human usage.

and with the media who may strongly influence that public judgment, then the decision must be made in the full glare of the
public limelight. It no longer suffices for me to call a group of
scientists to my office and, when we have finished, to announce
that based on their advice I have arrived at a certain decision.
Rather, it is necessary for me to lay my scientific evidence and
advice on the table where it may be examined and, indeed, cross-
examined by other scientists and the public alike before I make
a final decision.

I fully realize that my announcements calling a public hearing
on the fate of DDT and making the scientific advisory committee
report public in the case of 2,4,5-T and then calling a subsequent
public hearing has concerned some scientists. I fully understand
the scientist's desire to seek a quiet spot to contemplate and carefully work out rational solutions, as well as his distaste of the
hysteria that sometimes accompanies public discussion of environmental issues. However, the demands of a free and open society
will not permit such a luxury. My obligation is to make a public
accounting of my decision — to explain why I have taken or refused to take certain action. You, too, must participate in this
explanatory process, if it is to be successful. Regardless of whether
those who support the decision speak out, some of the opposition
to the action will be heard. And, all sides must be heard. Regardless of the emotion surrounding an issue, reason must prevail.
To fail to publicly support a wise decision may well be to concede
defeat in the battle to convince the public of the credibility of
the decision, and without such credibility, neither you nor I will
long be entrusted with decisions that the public considers vital
to their lives....

Attitudes and environmental problems — In the preceding pages the case
has been made that man is well on his way to destroying the as yet poorly
understood life support systems of this planet and that this is being done
without widespread public understanding of the potential consequences.
What should be done about this depends upon our attitudes toward ourselves, toward nature, and toward our progeny. Underlying the attitudes
are our basic ethical tenets.

In an interesting, recent article Cook (1970) identified three primary
ethical positions relative to the environment which he labeled the *development
ethic,* the *preservation ethic,* and the *equilibrium ethic.* Each of these ethical
positions has its own appropriate code of conduct against which ecological
morality may be measured.

The development ethic derives from orientation to action rather than
from contemplation. It unquestioningly assumes that man is and should
be master of nature, that the earth and its resources are here for man's
benefit and pleasure. This view is reinforced by the *work ethic* which dictates
that man should be busy with his hands, creating continual change; that

things which are bigger, better, and faster represent "progress" which is, of itself, good. If it can be done it should be done. Man's unbounded energy is best harnessed in creative work. This orientation is entirely compatible with religious doctrines which feature a "happy hunting ground" or "heavenly home" in the next life and which consider the earth to be just a proving ground.

The preservation ethic recognizes something special in nature itself, but the reasons for doing so range rather widely. At one end of the spectrum are adherents of certain oriental religions who believe in reincarnation as well as the modern day Druid-types who feel a mystical oneness with the universe and who would spell Nature with a capital "N." Closely akin are those who, like Albert Schweitzer, feel a "reverence for life." Applying the Golden Rule to all creatures (as products of the same Creator), they respect the right of all to live. As Noah was charged to be steward of nature, so should we. Other preservationists include those whose interest is primarily esthetic or recreational. Nature is beautiful; it is a tonic for man. It should be available for weekend picnics, hiking, canoeing, camping, hunting, fishing, or for just peace and quiet. Also among the preservationists are those whose reasons are essentially scientific. Man depends upon and has much to learn from nature. Rare and endangered species and ecosystems as well as the more common ones must be preserved because of their known or assumed long-range practical utility. In this view natural diversity, variety, complexity and wildness is held to be superior to humanized uniformity, sameness, simplicity, and domesticity.

The equilibrium ethic, which apparently stems from and is closely related to the scientific preservationist view mentioned above, extends its rational consideration to the entire earth and for all time. It recognizes the desirability of decent living standards, but it works toward a balance of resource use and resource availability. It exhorts mankind to develop a stable equilibrium with the environment — well short of disaster. It abhors rapid and uncontrolled growth in population and economy as being self-defeating in the long run. Because of its dimensions, this is essentially a new ethic whose only real shibboleth is survival, but this one consideration greatly overshadows all other moral, ethical, religious, political, and national goals. One people living together in one world — indefinitely.

Who Will Solve the Problems?

Civilization is a Greek tragedy based upon the development ethic, and the performance is nearly complete. The only way to avoid the intolerable inevitable is to change the ethical theme. Can it be done? Many professional ecologists have apparently given up hope. Among the others, whether hope has been abandoned or not, there is furious activity to accomplish what they can.

In the past few years, a number of important steps have been taken which suggest that the complex environmental problems can and will be handled effectively within the United States. Public indignation mounting at all levels has served notice that the environmental issue is volatile, that the feelings run deep, and that the matter is not one of passing interest. Establishment of the Council on Environmental Quality and the Environmental Protection Agency were movements in the right direction, as were a series of environmental protection bills passed by the federal and state legislatures. News media and the legal profession were quick to grasp the message, spread the word, and defend public rights. Environmental impact statements, now required in advance of major environmental modification projects, have slowed the pace of environmental deterioration and laid open for inspection the various value gains and losses so that all may understand and speak to the real issues. The cross-Florida barge canal, Central American sea-level canal, trans-Alaska pipeline, Miami jetport, the SST, and other potentially destructive projects have been stopped cold pending in-depth study.

Of especial note is the recent establishment of The Institute of Ecology under sponsorship of major educational and scientific institutions of the United States, Canada, and the Latin American nations. Under the auspices of the Institute, the collective expertise of the community of environmental scientists can quickly and effectively be brought to bear on wide-ranging environmental problems, some of which are of global magnitude. The voice of unbiased authority is now available to examine the alternatives, and the probability of understanding how to achieve equilibrium is immeasurably increased.

Perhaps most important is a general sense that many attitudes have changed. One no longer hears scornful officials dismiss ecologists as "bird watchers" and "communists." One seldom hears all industrialists branded as resource mongers and polluters. One doesn't hear ecologists advocating an end to all industry and a sigh for the good old caveman days. There are exceptions, but the trend now is for communication and understanding. There is considerable evidence that many municipalities and industries are making serious and costly efforts to create a better environment. A live-and-let-live philosophy is replacing the shootout, but the gun belts will not be hung up until a cleaner world has been achieved. This is not the time to relax our ecological vigilance.

Somewhat parallel developments are taking place in the developed nations throughout the world, both socialist and democratic, and the signs, again, are hopeful. The underdeveloped nations, at the moment, must decide between cleanliness and survival, but they are not the world's big polluters. Hopefully, if the population problem can be solved soon, even their cleanup can begin. Legislation cannot alone, however, provide for long-range and widespread environmental quality. What is really needed is change in the hearts of men — recognition that nature is friend, not foe, and support for a doctrine of dependence.

Mechanics of Environmental Problem Solving

The framework for day-to-day solving of environmental problems may be stated as follows. Man must make *use* of the environment, but in so doing he must preserve certain environmental *values*. Each use has an *impact* upon several values, but up to a certain point the use is nondestructive. Therefore, practical and definable limits must be set for use-impact for each environmental value.

The sense of this will be made clearer with an example. The water-quality engineer knows that most species of fishes will survive indefinitely if the oxygen level of a body of water remains above 4.0ppm. Below this point, troubles occur, depending upon the sensitivity of individual species, ambient temperature, presence of pollutants, and other factors. In order to preserve the value (in this case, the fishes) he must keep the level above the danger point, and he selects 5.0ppm as a safe point, providing some margin for error. The engineer knows that a number of human uses may place demands upon the oxygen supply. He, therefore, recommends that regardless of how the various uses may be allocated, the total impact of all uses cannot be allowed to pass the critical level of tolerance (set at 5.0ppm).

Passing now to the analysis of a complex environment, we examine the matrix of uses vs. environmental values (Figure 10.3). In this figure, many uses are considered in relation to many values. The impact of a given use upon several values may be studied, or one can focus upon the impacts of all uses upon a single value. In a real situation the individual impacts might represent numbers, ratios, or differential equations express-ing relationships of a series of variables. In the long run such matrix analy-ses can serve as the basis for computer models of the systems under study.

In approaching the use-impact-value equations it is helpful to realize that scientific knowledge and technological judgment enter into the deter-mination of critical levels of tolerance and magnitudes of impact of different uses. Social judgment enters into the determination of what value levels society is willing to pay for and how the various uses should be allocated within limits of tolerance of the systems. Acceptable impact levels, taken together, define what is called "environmental quality."

Rationing

Earlier in the chapter it was noted that long-range stability in the soci-ety-ecosystem complex depends upon establishment and maintenance of an acceptable level of environmental impact, and this has now been spelled

Values \ Uses	Env. value 1	Env. value 2	Env. value 3	. . . .	Env. value x
Use$_a$	impact$_{a/1}$	impact$_{a/2}$	impact$_{a/3}$	. . . .	impact$_{a/x}$
Use$_b$	impact$_{b/1}$	impact$_{b/2}$	impact$_{b/3}$	. . . .	impact$_{b/x}$
Use$_c$	impact$_{c/1}$	impact$_{c/2}$	impact$_{c/3}$	. . . .	impact$_{c/x}$
⋮	⋮	⋮	⋮	. . . . ⋮ . . .	⋮
Use$_n$	impact$_{n/1}$	impact$_{n/2}$	impact$_{n/3}$	. . . .	impact$_{n/x}$
Totals	($I_{a\text{-}n/1}$)	($I_{a\text{-}n/2}$)	($I_{a\text{-}n/3}$)	. . . .	($I_{a\text{-}n/x}$)

Figure 10.3. Matrix analysis of *use* vs. *environmental values.* The component impacts of each use are distributed among the values which they affect. The total impact of all uses upon a given value must not exceed a defined impact level if environmental quality is to be preserved.

out in terms of the various environmental values. It remains to be pointed out that this can only be achieved by some form of environmental rationing. The day is not far away when citizens will need a ration card and will have to await their turns to visit a national park, the seashore, a lake, or a river. Hunting, fishing, and boating privileges will have to be allocated. Building and use permits, permission to operate an automobile, and personal income restrictions will be features of life of persons already living today. A few years further down the road lies rationing of food, water, and other necessities of life. Beyond that, who knows?

Clearly, the democratic society cannot be expected to survive in a world where everything must be rationed and controlled. Can we stop somewhere short of such a world? Yes, we can, by restricting reproduction. We will either ration offspring or we will have to ration everything else. It is my belief that society will eventually face up to its responsibility to the children which are produced. Others are not so optimistic.

Suggestions for Further Reading

Cook, E. "Ecoethics, Environmental Politics, and Miner-Devils." *Mining Congress Journal,* September 1970.

Darling, F. F. et al. *Future Environments of North America.* Garden City, New York: Natural History Press, 1966.

EHRLICH, P. R.; HOLDREN, J. P.; and HOLM, R. W. *Man and the Ecosphere.* San Francisco: W. H. Freeman & Co., 1971.

EWALD, W. R., Jr. *Environment for Man: The Next Fifty Years.* Bloomington, Ind.: Indiana University Press, 1967.

HARDIN, G. *Population, Evolution and Birth Control.* San Francisco: W. H. Freeman & Co., 1969.

HARTE, J., and SOCOLOW, R. H. *Patient Earth.* New York: Holt, Rinehart and Winston, 1971.

McHARG, I. *Design with Nature.* Garden City, N.Y.: Natural History Press, 1969.

MACKAYE, B. *The New Exploration: A Philosophy of Regional Planning.* Bloomington, Ind.: Indiana University Press, 1967.

Ocean Science Committee of the Ocean Affairs Board, Report of Special Study Committee. *Marine Environmental Quality, Suggested Research Programs for Understanding Man's Effect on the Oceans.* Washington, D.C.: National Academy of Science — National Research Council, 1971.

ODUM, H. T. *Environment, Power, and Society.* New York: John Wiley & Sons, 1971.

TERNES, A. P. et al. "The State of the Species." *Natural History,* January 1970.

UDALL, S. *1976: Agenda for Tomorrow.* New York: Harcourt, Brace & World, 1968.

WILLIAMS, C. M. "Third Generation Pesticides." *Scientific American,* July 1967.

epilogue/a declaration
of dependence

When, in the course of human history, mankind is confronted with a train of crises which, if unresolved, will lead rapidly and unfailingly to progressive deterioration in the quality of human life, a decent respect to the rights of unborn generations compels examination of the basic causes of the crises, elaboration of courses of remedial action, and definition of the fundamental constraints under which society must thereafter be governed if it is to enjoy the good life in perpetuity.

To all observant men it is now abundantly evident that mankind can not dwell on this planet alone; that his continued success as a species rests in the recognition of man's partnership with Nature; that technology notwithstanding, man, as a creature of the earth, is bound within the mutualistic framework of the ecological systems of this planet. Nevertheless, man has heaped abuse upon Nature as though, by Divine right, he had dominion over the very framework through which he exists.

He has procreated without constraint so that the present level of the population already far exceeds the ability of the environment to support such human numbers on a sustained basis.

He has gorged himself upon the natural resources of the earth with the result that resource famine, already evident in many quarters, will eventually reduce men everywhere to the role of pitiful scavengers recombing the litter of a ravaged biosphere.

Through agricultural malpractice and concretization he has destroyed vast areas of the living soil so that it no longer brings forth productive abundance in season.

To the end of maximizing his own temporary profit and comfort he has despoiled the atmosphere, the soil, and the waters of the earth by wanton discard of the wastes of civilization.

He has devised, produced, and distributed throughout the environments of the world toxic and biologically indestructible chemical materials in such abundance that they accumulate and poison both himself and the other species of Nature.

He has invoked legal, economic, political, and Divine sanction for massive programs of environmental destruction which, by accident and by design, have resulted in the systematic annihilation of populations, races, and species of the nonhuman inhabitants of the earth.

Therefore, in consideration of the fact that free and uncontrolled pursuit of individual happiness is incompatible with the general welfare of the human and nonhuman inhabitants of this planet, and of the fact that continuance of the present trends will lead to the ultimate collapse of both

145

civilization and the remaining systems of Nature, be it now resolved that in thought and in deed man must recognize the rights and privileges of his cohabitants and his descendants. To secure and safeguard these rights he must proceed without delay to establish the legal, fiscal, and operational framework to limit the rate of human reproduction, to restrict the pace of resource depletion, to restore the fertility of the land, to recover and detoxify his own wastes, to establish a system of inviolate preserves wherein the silent species may find permanent haven and refuge, to reconstitute the disordered balance of Nature.

Lest the opportunity of restoring a balance pass forever by, highest priority must be given to the development of a master plan, global in scope, for setting the ecological house in order. Within this context programs for action must be developed and carried out at every administrative level. As a matter of individual and collective conscience man must realize that he cannot go it alone; that he must rapidly evolve from a consumer to a preserver society. Our generation shall either accept the challenge of redirecting the calamitous course of history or our wretched descendants shall thereafter hold us responsible for failure to do so.

index

*Page numbers in bold face refer to illustrations.